Ready, Set, Be Still

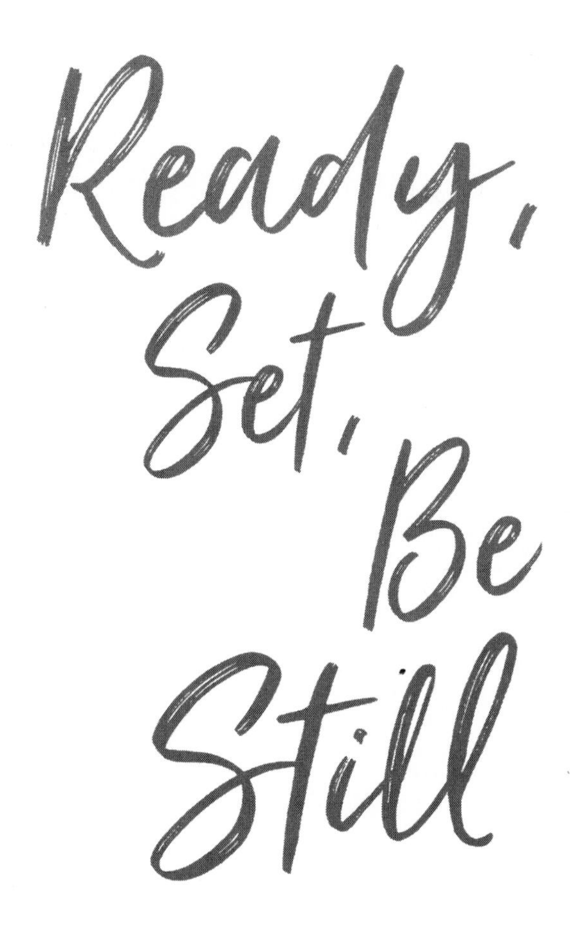

How GOD Used FAITH and Personal REVELATION to Transform My Life

FATIMA DEDRICKSON

CFI
An imprint of Cedar Fort, Inc.
Springville, Utah

ISBN 13: 978-1-4621-2310-0

Published by CFI, an imprint of Cedar Fort, Inc.
2373 W. 700 S., Springville, UT 84663
Distributed by Cedar Fort, Inc., www.cedarfort.com

LIBRARY OF CONGRESS CATALOGING-IN-PUBLICATION DATA

Names: Dedrickson, Fatima, 1989- author.
Title: Ready, set, be still : how God used faith and personal revelation to transform my life / Fatima Dedrickson.
Description: Springville, Utah : CFI, an imprint of Cedar Fort, Inc., [2019] | Includes bibliographical references and index.
Identifiers: LCCN 2018047968 (print) | LCCN 2018053866 (ebook) | ISBN 9781462129805 (epub, pdf, mobi) | ISBN 9781462123100 (perfect bound : alk. paper)
Subjects: LCSH: Dedrickson, Fatima, 1989- | Mormon women--Biography. | Christian life--Mormon authors. | LCGFT: Autobiographies.
Classification: LCC BX8695.D43 (ebook) | LCC BX8695.D43 A3 2019 (print) | DDC 289.3092 [B] --dc23
LC record available at https://lccn.loc.gov/2018047968

Cover design by Shawnda T. Craig
Cover design © 2019 Cedar Fort, Inc.
Edited by Kathryn Watkins, Melissa Caldwell, and Heather Holm
Typeset by Kaitlin Barwick

Printed in the United States of America

10 9 8 7 6 5 4 3 2 1

Printed on acid-free paper

To my husband and my children,
my mom and dad, my siblings,
and my in-laws!

To the Rasolos, the Welches, and the Taylors.

Thank you for loving me and
helping me become who I am today.

Contents

Introduction

I am Fatima, but you can call me Fatty, and this is my story.

If you want to know my story for real, you need to start at the *very* beginning—where I was born. That sounds super cliché, but it is really true in this case! I was born in a place that not a lot of you have ever been, unless you've served a mission there.

I was born in the beautiful city of Stockholm, Sweden, to parents from the Congo. They had migrated to Sweden a few years before to make a better life for their eight kids. Big families exist outside of the Church, everybody. Latter-day Saints don't have the monopoly on that. My dad had seventeen siblings, and my mom had twelve, so there's the proof right there! Can you imagine our family reunions? We used to have them in France or Belgium almost every summer growing up.

The Catholic Church is huge in Congo, so that's how my parents grew up. They'd never even heard about The Church of Jesus Christ of Latter-day Saints until they moved to Sweden, but it didn't take long. My dad is a total social butterfly. Everybody knows him and loves him. And how can you not?

This is how my dad introduces himself, every time without fail: "I'm Fidel. But not Fidel like Fidel Castro. Fidel Makakala." You can see why he was a popular guy.

Not long after moving to Sweden, he met the missionaries on the train and immediately started chatting them up. Pretty soon, he started taking the discussions, though my mom wasn't quite ready for that yet. They went to separate churches for a little while, my dad going to The Church of Jesus Christ and my mom still attending the local Catholic church. Her curiosity got the better of her, though, and she started taking the discussions too and got baptized.

A year later, they were sealed in the Stockholm Sweden Temple, two months after I was born. I obviously can't remember that day, but I smile at the image of all of us trying to fit in the sealing room. And then tears fill my eyes at the image of *all* of us fitting in that sealing room, the idea of all ten of us being together

"I note the obvious differences
between each sort and type,
but we are more alike, my friends,
than we are unalike."

—"Human Family," a poem by Maya Angelou

forever. That's what that day represents to me. A family becoming eternal.

Growing up in Stockholm, I was one of four members of The Church of Jesus Christ of Latter-day Saints in my high school. That shows you how small the Church membership is there. My high school was the only one in the area, so most kids went there. In the United States, there are so many schools everywhere that it is easy to forget that other countries aren't the same.

Being one of the very few members wasn't too hard for me, because back then the worst thing people did was smoke, and none of my friends did that. I must say my parents taught us well and were very firm with our rules at home. That taught us that if someone was doing something we did not believe in, we didn't need to participate.

My parents also knew all of our friends. They truly made an effort to get to know them. That way they knew who we were hanging out with. Besides, if my parents loved who I was hanging out with, then they were more willing to let me stay out late—win win!

All of us kids played sports, except my three older sisters. In our house, you either ran track or played basketball. That was it! Besides the gospel, those were our religions. Now that I'm older, I totally understand why my mom wanted us to do our own laundry back then! But back then, it was the worst thing ever.

I was driven by sports from a young age. My parents say I had too much energy, and that's why they put me in soccer. I'm so thankful for their intuition, because I discovered not only my natural ability, but also my drive to succeed and to improve. My days were consumed with either soccer or track and, at the end of the day, sweaty socks and shorts that, for some reason, my mom didn't want to deal with. Rude.

A less sweaty and much cleaner skill that I picked up on was my passion for languages. I grew up trilingual, speaking Swedish at school and French and Lingala at home. If that wasn't enough, I also took seven years of Spanish in school, plus a little bit of English, but I really didn't know much. I was going to regret not learning more English when I went to college.

So that's a snapshot of me! A Swedish member of The Church of Jesus Christ of Latter-day Saints, a lover of food, and a multilingual athlete with tons of siblings and a huge extended family. Fatty in a nutshell.

We all have descriptors that identify us and make us unique. But odds are that you read that list and found something that you and I have in common! That's great! From the surface, it might look like I'm way different from you and how you grew up, but when you get to know me (and when you get to know anyone, really) you'll realize that we are a lot more alike than we are different. So grab a chocolate chip cookie, and let's go on this ride together, because that's what life is all about: cookies and togetherness.

Feel free to quote me on that.

Cookies and togetherness

It's what life is all about.

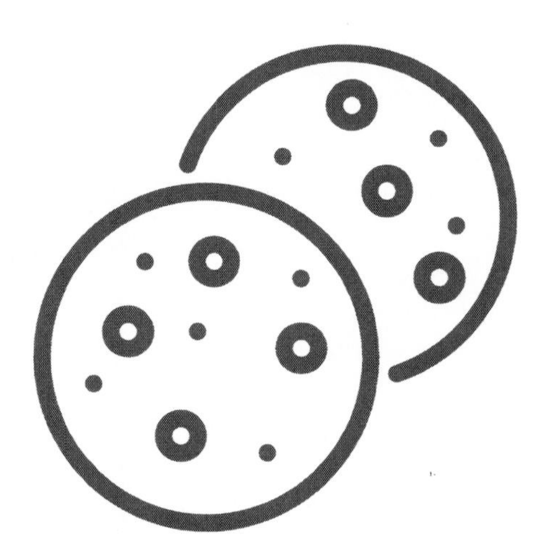

—Fatima Dedrickson

Chapter 1

Life in Sweden

My house was like a way station. My parents (99 percent my mom) constantly invited people into our home. There were always people coming and going. The Makakala house was definitely the place where friends and even strangers came to hang out, have a meal, and even sleep over. Sometimes I was annoyed when I had to share a room with my little sisters because I had given up my room so another person or family could use it to sleep. I knew it was nice, but I still didn't really understand it. Do you know what I mean? Like when you're a kid and you know you're supposed to do something, but you don't know why?

One day I asked my mom, "Why do you let strangers stay in our home?" I thought surely she would see that I was being inconvenienced and give me my room back.

She would understand that family came first and no one else should be allowed to sleep in my bed except me! But that's not what she said, believe it or not. She hugged me tight, looked me in the eyes, and said, "Because one day, I might not be here. And I hope someone will do the same for my family."

Well then. I was instantly humbled by her kindness.

She taught me that day, and every day since, that what goes around comes around. She expected me to learn to love my neighbor and to see others as God's children. Because one day, I would want someone to extend to me that same love and kindness. It was not a question of *if*, but *when*. And it would be a lot easier to ask for it if I had first given it.

Though I couldn't quite wrap my head around it yet, I tried to think of what it would be like to not have a bed of my own. It helped me so that when I sometimes gave mine up, I definitely knew I would get it back when that family moved on. If I didn't have one *at all,* I truly didn't know what that would feel like. It was a lot easier to give up my bed after that.

My mom raised her kids to be kind and charitable, and like I said earlier, there are a lot of us. So I was raised in this environment of kindness and sacrifice. Imagine my surprise when I got to school and not everyone was as nice as my mom. I was the youngest in my class because I had skipped a grade. As if that weren't hard enough on its own, in Sweden, the school system doesn't really ease you into school like in America. There's no preschool. There's one program that you start when you are eighteen months old and you stay in until you're five. It's basically day care. Once you turn five, you start school. Not much of a transition, right? And that was hard on little Fatima.

My mom worked full time, so my older siblings helped raise me pretty much. My teachers thought my older sister, Nicole, was my mom, because she was always the one picking me up from school and dropping me off. I didn't think that was weird or anything. It was all I knew. My mom had always worked full time, so it wasn't hard for me. She did what she had to do to support me and to feed her large family. And I always knew that she loved me and had my back.

My Dad worked as well. He traveled back and forth to Africa a lot, which was hard for us but also made our family closer and meant that my brothers were the men in the house!

When I look back at that time, I understand a lot more about my mom—what she was going through and what she must have felt trying to provide for so many kids, not only financially but also emotionally. I know it was hard. But she never let it show. She always saw the good in me, even when I didn't see it. But I learned that year that not everyone would see the good in me like she did.

What's a little bit scary to me is how much I forgot about my own bullying experiences until I started writing this. You don't really realize the things kids go through or remember everything you went through when you were young and in school. I look back on my early schoolyard experiences with bullying, and I get scared for my kids and the bullying that they, unfortunately, will inevitably experience. I only hope I can love them like my mother loved me, so much that they know it without question and so much that when they feel a lack of love from any other source, it will feel wrong to them because of how much they are loved at home.

Anyway, when I was six, I switched schools. I went to a French-immersion school an hour away from where I lived. Oh boy, was it hard! The teachers were all from France, and we were not allowed to speak Swedish. I don't remember speaking Swedish even once during all my time at that school.

It was extremely hard, but I learned to be disciplined in my studies. As a result, I learned to speak and write in French on a very high level, and that has served me well throughout my life, even at BYU. That school year was full of personal growth for me, not all of it comfortable. I went on super awesome school trips to other countries like Spain, Belgium, and France. But I also started being more involved in sports besides soccer.

For instance, I did run a lot in school, but for the first time, I ran "long distance" at this school. Basically,

STAND UP

FOR WHAT IS

RIGHT

EVEN IF YOU STAND

ALONE

I ran long races that I absolutely *hated*, which was frustrating for me. I was one of those athletic kids. I was always moving around and running around. Physical activities came easily to me, so I was super frustrated to have this new activity that I didn't like and that wasn't easy right off the bat. Have you ever had something like that happen? Say there's something that you use to define yourself, like being good at sports. It happens a lot at school, like, "This is Fatty. She's good at sports." Or "Let's pick Fatty for our team because she's good at sports," but then you're not good at *every* sport and you feel like a fraud?

Or maybe you aren't good at sports after all? That's always frustrating and an experience that we all have to deal with. You decide how you're going to come out of that. For me, I learned that I *loved* sprinting! Long distance is the worst, and no one can tell me any different. Why slog through miles when you can fly? My parents saw that and enrolled me in track when I turned eight. I thank them for that all the time. It might seem weird, but track has saved me in so many aspects of my life.

That year was one of the hardest years I had ever had socially as well. Prior to that year, I had been in the same school, with the same classmates and the same friends. There were new people here and there, but mostly it was the same. So adjusting to a new school, a new language, *and* new friends was just a triple whammy. But what really hurt my little heart and soul at that school was the bullying I saw and experienced. The worst of it revolved around a girl in my class who was really quiet. She had such a hard time fitting in, but she tried her best. That's always the most heartbreaking part. She tried so hard.

One day, I saw a couple of the other girls feed her mud. I was in shock and so horrified. I couldn't believe what I was seeing. I remember running to her and trying to help, but she was so embarrassed that she pushed me away. My heart hurt for her, but I think I would've reacted the same way. Even though she was very different from me and we didn't really have much in common, I stood up for her that day and every day after. And I made sure she was never alone.

Because I did that for her, the girls tried to gang up on me too. I lost a lot of friends. That was really hard. It's always hard to lose people you thought were your friends for doing what you know is right. But in the end, it was okay because I gained a lot of new friends too. You win some, you lose some. But I would never go back and not stand up for that girl, because bullying is never okay, no matter how old you are. I guess it goes back to what my mom taught me: what goes around comes around, and we should always stick together. I was no stranger to bullying, so when I saw that girl in the mud, it was like watching myself.

Growing up, I was always smaller, thinner, and more muscular than the other girls, and they made fun of me because of that. I learned at that age (eleven or so) to be self-conscious about my body. I thought it was manly to have arms and legs that were muscly and that I was made wrong.

No little girl or boy should ever feel like they were made wrong! But so many of them do. I believe that when people belittle and demean others, they do it because they aren't happy with themselves. They think they will feel better if they can give the pain they feel to others. But really, all they're doing is spreading it around. Creating more of it. And that's heartbreaking.

To get myself out of that cycle, I asked my parents to switch schools, and that's what we did. The school I switched to was in my neighborhood, and all of my friends went there. But I was so nervous. I had been going to this French-immersion school, and I felt like I would be totally behind. And it was true. I was behind in Swedish and English. That year they added foreign language studies. I was doomed. But God gave me an angel in human form to get me through it all—a Swedish seventh grader named Rakeb.

I met her on the first day of seventh grade, and to this day, eighteen years later, she is still one of my best friends. When I say "met," that isn't entirely true. I had met Rakeb before. Here's how it went: there was a girl who lived in Rakeb's neighborhood whose family attended church, but sporadically. I was friends with that girl. She was friends with Rakeb. So when I would play at the park with my friend, I would see Rakeb. I never really *knew* her until that day in school.

I saw her and she saw me, and we did "The Nod" from across the room. You know the one. The one that's like saying, "Yeah, I know you." And I could tell we were thinking the same thing: "I have a friend here." And the rest is history.

It was so long ago and so instinctual that I barely remember the details, honestly. She's kind of on the shy side, and I am very much not anywhere near that side, so you wouldn't think that we would work, but it was just easy to be her friend. She is the kind of friend that everyone wants and should have. She is someone that I have always been able to count on, no matter what. Ever since that first day, when I felt like my life was over at thirteen years old, Rakeb has been there. We did everything together. We traveled all over Europe together. I would say, "Let's go to London this weekend," and we'd go to London! If it sounds like a fairy tale, that's kind of what it felt like! We made so many memories seeing the world together. We played on the same soccer team, and we were a great team on the field as well as off. She was my rock. And I wasn't the only one who loved her and knew how good she was. I could ask my parents, "Can I go to such and such a place? I'm going with Rakeb," and I knew they would say yes, no questions asked. She has become more like a sister to me than anything. She flew from Sweden to meet each

"We cannot tell the
precise moment when friendship
is formed. As in filling a vessel drop
by drop, there is at last a drop which
makes it run over; so in a series of
kindnesses there is at last one which
makes the heart run over."

—James Boswell,
The Life of Samuel Johnson, LL.D

of my children when they were born. She has literally come every year to visit my family.

When I needed a familiar face while I was attending BYU, she flew all the way to Utah. She's one of the most wonderful people I know. I can count on one hand the number of times I've been mad at her. We've had maybe one fight. And even if that one fight exists, I can't for the life of me remember what it would have been about. My kids call her Auntie Rakeb. We talk every other day, if not every day. Sometimes we go a little bit longer between FaceTiming, but we understand that that's life sometimes, and when we are able to talk again, it's like no time passed. Our families are even best friends! Isn't that like something off a TV show? The best friends whose families are like family?

I consider myself so lucky to have someone like Rakeb and to have met her when I needed her the most. God knew what He was doing putting those two seventh graders together. She made the difference for me that day, that year, and for the rest of my life. I can't imagine what my life, and the lives of my kids, would be like without her! I learned that a situation is never as bad as it seems, especially when you have a great friend to go through it with. Rakeb changed my whole outlook, my whole experience.

And I learned that I can be that difference for someone too. Rakeb needed a friend as badly as I needed one. We helped each other. Any one of us can make a difference for someone. We just have to be looking out, being all in and humble enough to see the difficulties of others. When you are having a hard time, look for someone else in a similar situation. Maybe, like Rakeb, you can end up lifting two people instead of just one.

Chapter 2

A Prompting I Really Wanted to Ignore

No matter who you are or where you live in the world, being a teenager is hard. When I was fifteen, I thought being a teenager was a special hell that I was going through alone. I think we've all felt that way, especially at that age. That no one knows exactly what we're going through. Heck, *I* didn't even know exactly what I was going through!

If I had to describe that age in one word, it would be "questions." Actually, I would describe it as "???," which I think of as more of a sound than anything else. Kind of like that little whine that a dog makes when it is confused and does that cute head tilt.

I had so many questions about who I was, who I would and should be, what I was doing, what I wanted, and so on. And I didn't feel like I had the answers to any of them. Even worse, there didn't seem to be a way to get the answers I needed. How do you find out who you are, really? You have to live life and experience things in order to really figure that out, but everything is so immediate when you're a teenager. You want to know everything yesterday so that you can get on with your life. Am I right?

Harold B. Lee described it pretty well in a comment to Boyd K. Packer. Elder Lee said, "'The trouble is you want to see the end from the beginning.' [Boyd K. Packer] replied that [he] would like to see at least a step or two ahead."[1] That's what being a teenager feels like. You know what you want life to be like, more or less; you know what you want to accomplish. And you can vaguely see the road there, but the first step is hidden from you. You know that if you could just start, then you'd get the hang of it and get there in no time. So why is it so hard to start?

That's where I was when I was fifteen. I felt all kinds of stuck and confused. At that time, I didn't have many friends at church. I didn't hang out with my ward friends on a daily basis. I hung out with my teammates and

1. Boyd K. Packer, "The Edge of the Light," BYU fireside address, 4 March 1990; adapted in *BYU Today* 45, no. 2 (March 1991), 22–24, 38–43.

stuff. So my gospel exposure was maybe a once-a-week thing, and I say "maybe" because track competitions were often held on weekends. I was getting very little exposure to what had the power to actually answer my questions! And that was part of the problem.

The Church and me? We weren't exactly tight. I had questions about the gospel. I had thoughts like, *Is this true? Am I doing the right things? Do I really believe in these things?* Any time I would actually think the questions, I would push them away. I would ignore them because they felt too big to deal with.

Until one particular day.

I remember I was going to practice or to a meet (was I ever going anywhere else?) and I looked out the window. I was feeling frustrated. So I decided to try a thought experiment. I thought to myself, *I don't believe in this [the gospel].* As soon as I said that in my mind, a really bad feeling flooded me. I felt awful, like I had lied. Immediately, I thought, *I take it back! I take it back!* and the feeling went away. I knew that I believed in the gospel.

But that didn't mean that I didn't have questions that I needed to ask. Nor did I get the answers the minute I asked. Sometimes answers come quickly, and sometimes they don't. And it is hard to keep the faith when you are going through trials. Be patient. Truth will come.

I continued on, more or less, in the same vein for a few more months. Then I had an interview with my bishop, right before I was to get my patriarchal blessing.

Wait

ON THE LORD:

Be of good COURAGE,

And He shall

STRENGTHEN

thine heart:

Wait,

I say, on the LORD.

PSALM 27:14

I remember sitting in his office, looking around at the walls during one of the periods of silence that happens during a bishop interview. I saw a picture of President Monson (then second counselor in the First Presidency) on the wall and thought, *I know nothing about him.* I felt absolutely no connection to him like I did to President Hinckley. That felt important to me. I felt not quite bummed, but more like, "One day I want to go to the Conference Center and feel it and really listen."

General conference is really different outside of the United States. Members who live in the same country as the prophets don't understand what it's like to be so far away from them. We have TV, radio, live stream, the Church magazines—all of that. So we hear what they say, but there's just something about knowing that they're close.

I could only imagine it. All of the missionaries that served in Sweden were basically from Utah. They all had amazing stories about conference and about literally living in Salt Lake City, in the same city as so many of the prophets. You have this fantasy almost. You fantasize about what it would be like to live in modern-day Zion. Can you imagine what that would be like, especially for someone who knew very few members? There are 9,701 members of The Church of Jesus Christ of Latter-day Saints in Sweden[2] versus 2,090,401 in Utah alone,[3] just for reference. I have lived in both places, and it is amazing how quickly I took it for granted when I lived in Utah. I could justify not going to general conference because there would be a face-to-face with a General Authority in a month, or my stake conference would have a visiting Seventy. I lived five minutes from the temple when I lived at Wyview in Provo.

But there was a time when I would have done anything to have experiences like that. Sweden has one temple, and we had to travel over one hour on public transportation to do the work for our families. And appearances from General Authorities rarely happen in Scandinavia. Count your many blessings.

With stories of general conference in my head, I knew that if I could just see President Monson speak, my testimony would be strengthened and I would be planted firmly on the path. But, as I said, Apostles very rarely came to Scandinavia. So imagine my surprise when one Sunday the bishop announced that there would be a special fireside address given by a General Authority. Here, in Sweden! I was electrified. A prophet of God could help me see the first steps! I wrote the date down in my

2. "Facts and Statistics: Sweden," *Newsroom*, https://www.mormonnewsroom.org/facts-and-statistics/country/sweden.
3. "Facts and Statistics: Utah," *Newsroom*, https://www.mormonnewsroom.org/facts-and-statistics/country/united-states/state/utah.

Church notebook and promised myself then and there that I wouldn't miss it for the world.

The day came, a Saturday evening. Something came up and my family decided not to go. It was a ways away, but I had made myself a promise, so I commuted alone. When I arrived, I was shocked. I had never seen the chapel so packed. People were there from all over Scandinavia, there to hear the words of the Lord's prophet. This was amazing to me, because prior to this day, I had never really felt connected with the prophet. I was used to watching firesides and general conference on a big screen. While I knew these men and women and I sustained them, they didn't feel totally real. As a result, I was never that serious about watching general conference and—I'll be honest—I had no idea there were Saturday sessions.

In spite of all this, I had a sincere desire to feel *something*. Anything. Like the hundreds of people from all over the country who were sitting in the seats already. So I went in and sat on the hard metal chairs (because all of the soft, cushiony ones were taken), and I took out the same journal where I had written "President Monson. Fireside. Saturday. GO! NO MATTER WHAT!" It was almost like a mini general conference for me.

A few years before, President Hinckley had come to Sweden, but I wasn't able to go. This was going to be my one chance. I didn't necessarily go there to have all of my questions answered, because that wasn't realistic. I just couldn't miss the opportunity. I just wanted to feel something! And if he answered any of my questions, so much the better. So I sat there, just waiting. For what, I didn't exactly know. But I believed that something would happen.

President Monson was sitting on the stand. It was so strange to see the face I had so often seen on TV right in front of me in real life. Our opening hymn was "We Thank Thee, O God, for a Prophet." We stood and sang as a congregation. When we sang to him, I had chills all over my body. Right then and there I knew with my whole heart that President Monson was a true prophet and that the connection I had been searching and praying for was there. Undeniable. The prayer of my heart was answered in the opening hymn! Meeting him wasn't necessary—I already knew what I needed to know.

But the experiences didn't end there.

That was the first time I ever actually took notes at a fireside. It was the first time I went to a fireside, or any church meeting, on a Saturday *by myself.* The first time I felt the Spirit so strongly that there was no way I could deny it. By the end of the hour, I had filled two pages of notes full of answers to my questions, where before I could barely pay attention to one speaker. Now *that's* a miracle!

After the program was over and the fireside officially ended, President Monson, being the humble and loving man that he was, decided he was going to shake hands with whoever got in line. It was already pretty late, but I knew that this was probably the only chance I would ever get to meet him face to face.

My heart was pounding, my hands were sweaty (no mom's spaghetti, thankfully), but I had made up my mind: I was not going to leave the line no matter how long it would take. I stood for over an hour, but once I got up to him, all the time melted away and it felt like seconds had passed. When I stood in front of him, time stood still. He took my hand in both of his, looked me straight in the eyes, and said in the voice I knew so well, "You are so beautiful, and we need you in Utah." I think I squeaked out a "Thank you." Then he smiled his beautiful, warm smile . . . and that was it.

You're probably thinking, *What do you mean "That was it," Fatty?!?*

The truth is, I was blown away. He said ten words to me and rocked me to my core.

Not only did he call me beautiful, but he also said I was needed in Utah! *What on earth could that mean?* I can roll my eyes at young Fatty now, but she was in total turmoil at those ten words.

When I finally got home that night, my thoughts were racing a million miles an hour. *What did that even mean? Did it even mean anything? I'm probably overreacting. He probably said that to everyone! . . . Right?* So many questions, but no answers just yet.

Despite the immediate inner turmoil of that night, I was able to shake it off for the most part and get on with day-to-day life. I graduated high school, and my graduation present was a trip to America, specifically to visit family in Boston and friends in Utah. I was absolutely thrilled to go, but there was only one problem. I didn't speak a lick of English! But, never one to shy away from a challenge, and because I had always wanted to go, I hopped on the plane to Utah.

I went there first to visit some family friends who just so happened to be students at—you guessed it—BYU. I had absolutely no desire to see the campus, but they insisted. So off to BYU I went. Once there, I happened to run into Anders, who was also from Sweden, and his children were BYU track athletes. He showed me around and then walked me to the track offices, where I met some student athletes, as well as Coaches Poole and Legas. You can see where this is going, right? I have no idea what I even told them, or how we communicated at all, but by the end of our "chat," I was walking out of their office with my arms filled with paperwork.

You might be able to see where this is headed, but I sure as heck didn't! I left with even more questions than I had when I came. *This can't be what President Monson was talking about, can it? I can't come to Utah! I can't even speak English! How could I possibly go to BYU and study? There's no way I can do this!*

Here's the thing—there's always a way. His way. Heavenly Father's plan is perfect, and if we trust in Him and His timing, everything will work out. I was doing a great job of that, obviously, so I know what I'm talking about.

Definitely a joke. I had no idea what to do and if it would work out. I have never prayed so much in my entire life as I did during that time. Every time I prayed, I asked Heavenly Father to send me somewhere else—unless this was His plan. I only included that last part because I knew I was supposed to. I so did *not* want this to be His plan. I knew deep down that it was, but I wasn't ready to face it. I can look back on the decision now and have the benefit of knowing that it would work out, but then I was stepping out purely on faith. Like Dr. Martin Luther King Jr. said, "Take the first step in faith. You don't have to see the whole staircase, just take the first step."[4] I really wanted to see the whole staircase before I took that step, though, is the thing.

The path I was being led to would require *a lot* from me. A lot of growth and stretching, and some of it looked like it would definitely be painful. And when

---

4. Martin Luther King Jr., as quoted in *Mother Jones Magazine* 16, no. 3 (May–June 1991), 77.

"TAKE THE FIRST STEP IN FAITH. YOU DON'T HAVE TO SEE THE WHOLE STAIRCASE, JUST TAKE THE FIRST STEP."

–Martin Luther King Jr.

you're about to make a huge choice like that, it's the painful stretching that you see, not the results of what you will become. Because you don't know what that looks like!

If sixteen-year-old Fatty ran into present-day Fatty on the street, would she even recognize herself? I'm willing to bet that she wouldn't. Because through Heavenly Father, we are capable of so much more growth and achievement than we think is possible. And the hardest part is probably overcoming the ideas we have in our own heads about what we can and can't do. I decided that I didn't want to be limited by my ideas of my abilities, so I booked a one-way ticket to Utah.

Chapter 3

UTAH-BOUND

I was definitely going to Utah, but BYU was still not on my radar. I wasn't convinced that was part of the staircase. But I became really good friends with a group of around eight missionaries, all from Utah, of course. I went to Institute and hung out with them all the time. Because they all lived in Utah, they all went to BYU, UVU, or the U of U. One of those schools. So they were all on board with their Swedish buddy going to a "local" college.

One of the sisters jokingly (or maybe she was serious) said, "If you come, maybe we can be neighbors—unless I'm married. That would be awkward, haha!"

One elder said, "You should go to BYU and run track. You will kill it there."

My parents were sold too. "Heck yeah! Go to BYU! That'll be awesome! You can get a scholarship and get a degree!"

So everyone was rooting for it except me.

Because I had one big problem. I wasn't happy running track anymore. I was nannying, and I loved that, but running track full time was hard with my job. My schedule looked like this: wake up, eat breakfast, go out for morning training, nanny, go work out again, eat dinner really fast, go to practice, bed time.

Lather, rinse, repeat.

Needless to say, I had a lot going on. Track wasn't fun anymore. It was like a chore or a job. I wasn't getting anything from it, and the thought of running for university filled me with dread. So despite how wonderful everyone was telling me it would be to run track at BYU, I wasn't on board.

It's crazy, but I was preparing all of this stuff, but still hoping that the Lord would send me somewhere else. I wasn't 100 percent committed. I was more like a petulant teen who wanted to go to Disneyland but was going on a road trip their parents wanted instead: "Okay, fine!"

So I was going through the motions, but I definitely wasn't happy about it. It was a weird time to be Fatty. My relationship with track notwithstanding, it was my best shot at getting into a school, so I had to keep up with it. Ugh.

I was in the middle of the season, and if I was going to BYU (or somewhere else, fingers crossed), then I needed to keep my times up. That season was not my best, let's just say that. And after that season, I *really* didn't want to go. I was using track as an excuse, though. There were a lot of reasons why leaving was scary.

I don't think people understand when I say that I'm *close* to my family. I am *close* to my family. We are so tight. We did everything together. We grew up together. My older sisters raised me, for crying out loud! Then I raised my younger sisters. The thought of leaving them for so long and being so far away was almost unbearable. I thought about it as little as possible. But my ticket was already bought.

I bought that ticket before I had taken the SAT, even before I had my visa. In order to get into the country, I needed a visa. In order to pay for BYU's tuition, I needed a scholarship. In order to get that scholarship, I had to pass the SAT. English isn't even my third language, so I knew this was going to be the most difficult test I had ever taken. So I had to pass an already incredibly difficult test—in a foreign language—in order to secure a scholarship to attend a college that I wasn't even fully accepted to yet, in a country that I wasn't legally allowed into yet, all on a prompting from Heavenly Father.

Can you say leap of faith?

I didn't just need a miracle for this all to work out. I needed a series of miracles, large and small. But first, I needed to put in the work.

I studied my butt off for the SAT. I prayed a ton too. I had faith that if this was Heavenly Father's plan, my work would pay off and I would pass. If I was supposed to be in Utah, it would happen! I walked around with an SAT prep book for about six months and studied vocabulary words that no one I knew understood either. The amount of prayers I said was unbelievable. When my eyes weren't closed in fervent prayer, they were glued to English vocab lists, practice math problems, and science questions.

I took the test in May, and I was supposed to move to Utah in August. I felt like I guessed on every question, except for the math portion. I killed the math section, which was the only part of the test I was confident that I had done well in. Everything else was up in the air, so I went home, said another prayer, and then settled in for the waiting game.

I wasn't sitting there twiddling my thumbs though. Not by a long shot. I still had tests to take and shots to get (my favorite—not!), and I had to get my I-20 so that I could enter the United States, and so on. I was so grateful for friends like Jacqueline, who was going through the same process, but for BYU–Hawaii, who helped me through the frustrating legal hurdles. It's hard to get into

I didn't just need a *miracle*
for this all to work out—
I needed a *series* of miracles,
LARGE AND *small.*

But first, I needed to
put in the work.

the United States, guys. And I was only getting clearance to study there. But that is a topic for another time.

At the time I was getting my ducks in a row for BYU, track was in full swing, and I was traveling all over Sweden almost every weekend. Because of all the away competitions, I rarely had time to go to church services or activities. That took a toll on me spiritually, but I knew that I needed to rely on Heavenly Father if I was going to make it, so I did things to compensate. I read the scriptures on the bus to meets. I was praying constantly—that wasn't an issue. Finding time to listen and be still, that was a struggle. But even if it was a few minutes on the bus or before a race, those precious moments of stillness were exactly what I needed when my personal life felt so much like a loud, crazy whirlwind!

The whirlwind came to end, though. In June, I got my SAT results back and . . . I passed!

Barely, mind you, but I passed, which meant that I had my scholarship and I was officially attending Brigham Young University as part of the incoming freshman class of 2008. Whew!

With school all figured out (for now), the only things I had left to do were to find housing and figure out my I-20.

Easier said than done.

The days were going by, and I still didn't have anything figured out for housing. I was resigned to showering in and sleeping on a bench in the track locker room when one weekend, out of the blue, I felt a prompting to cancel the track meet I was going to and stay home. I thought to myself, *Sounds weird, but okay.* I decided to go to Institute instead, which I'm pretty sure was the first time I'd gone in months. And get this—when I showed up that day, the BYU Swedish teacher and his class happened to be there. I talked to them about the school since I would be going there, and we chatted back and forth for a bit. As we talked about my plans for school, it came out that I still didn't have a place to live. It went a little something like this:

"I teach in the Swedish department at BYU."

"Wow! That's so cool! I'll be going to BYU in the fall."

"Well, you'll definitely have to come to our class or come over for dinner when you're at school. Where will you be living? On campus or in your own apartment?"

"I don't know yet! I've been looking, but finding housing there is really difficult. I haven't found a place yet."

"Well, you are welcome to stay with us while you are looking. My wife is from France, so she knows how it is."

My jaw about hit the floor. I could not believe that they offered to let me, a total stranger, live in their home. But then I remembered the prompting I had received earlier in the day, and suddenly it didn't seem like such an incredible, unbelievable coincidence anymore. Heavenly Father had led me to this man who had a heart open to help a stranger in need, who had the language skills to communicate with me, easing my anxieties about the language barrier, at least for a while.

I was overwhelmed by his kindness. All I could do was smile so hard my cheeks hurt and give him my sincere thanks.

And just like that, I had somewhere to stay. All that was left was my visa.

My appointment at the visa office was set only one week before my flight to America. And I had booked a one-way ticket with no travel insurance, so there was no way to cancel if anything didn't work out. Needless to say, I was a stressed-out mess. In the weeks leading up to that appointment, I was mentally trying to figure out how I was going to tell my parents that the money for the ticket was gone, down the drain.

One Sunday, two weeks before my original appointment, I felt a nudge to go check the website and see if anyone had canceled their appointment. I shrugged it off as a random thought and kept doing what I was doing, but I was stopped dead when the prompting came again, but stronger this time: *Go check online now.*

I couldn't shrug *that* off, so I ran to the computer, got on the website, and saw one new open spot. I have never moved my fingers as quickly as I did to book that appointment.

When I got the confirmation for my new appointment, three weeks before my flight instead of one, I

When one door of happiness
CLOSES, another OPENS;
but often we look so long at the closed
door that we DO NOT SEE the one which
HAS BEEN OPENED FOR US.

—Alexander Graham Bell

laughed out of sheer relief. Then I cried and laughed some more. I had a lot of emotions rolling through me in that moment, but one thing I felt above all else was that the miracles I had prayed for to get me to Utah were happening.

I'm giving you the highlights here, but the day to day of this Hail Mary to BYU was so crazy. So many times I felt discouraged and overwhelmed—that I wouldn't pass the SAT no matter how hard I studied, that my visa wouldn't go through, and that I wouldn't find housing. I doubted myself and questioned the promptings I had received. I went so far as to ask myself, "Is this really right? Is all of this just in my head? Am I just wasting my time and money on something that will never happen?"

But every time those nagging doubts burrowed into my mind and put knots in my stomach, I remembered that handshake and the words of President Monson. And I remembered the Spirit I felt that day. I could not deny in that moment that I was being called to Utah.

Besides my own testimony of this experience, God sent me little blessings and miracles along the way, right when I needed them or when I was just about to give up, as signs to show me that it was time to go. There were many times I was ready to give up, because I honestly thought there was no way it would all work out. And then the doctor's appointment would be scheduled. The test would work out. *It would work out.*

There is always a way. His way. Trust in Him, in His timing, and in the witnesses He has given you, and things will always work out.

Goodbye, Sweden.

Utah, here I come!

Chapter 4

Goodbye, Sweden

No one tells you that this part will be the hardest. You don't really realize how many people you know until you move, am I right?! Suddenly I was saying goodbye to a ton of people I had become close to over the years.

My best friends from track threw me a goodbye party. Who invented those, by the way? Parties are supposed to fun. You're not supposed to be crying through the entire thing. But I was glad to see them all one last time. We reminisced about all of the shenanigans we got up to on the bus between meets, at practice, at school—all that stuff. That was the definition of bittersweet.

I had friends come over the week before my flight to say goodbye to me. My track besties (Sofia and Paulina) made me a pillowcase with a picture of us so that I could see them before I went to bed. I'm tearing up just thinking about it. Those kinds of things are great, because you are reminded what great friends you have . . . right before you fly thousands of miles away from them.

As hard as that was, saying goodbye to my family is, to this day, one of the saddest goodbyes I have ever said. My dad gave me a father's blessing before I left. I cherish and think of that blessing often. I had to say goodbye to my mom early, because she had to work and couldn't come to the airport. She hugged me so tight and said, "Do your part with faith, and Heavenly Father will do His."

I cried all the way to the airport, but I still got on the plane, ready to do my part. It didn't really hit me until I was letting go of my dad and turning my back to my little sisters to get on the plane. My little sisters were my two little shadows. They had followed me everywhere from the moment they could crawl, but even more so when they could walk. We were best friends, and it broke my heart to leave them behind.

I cried for most of the sixteen-hour flight to Utah. I knew I was following the Lord's path for me—don't get me wrong. I knew I was leaving for the right reasons and that I needed to leave in order to become what I needed to become. That doesn't mean it wasn't hard to leave my safe harbor and my family. I grieved for the closeness I wouldn't feel for I didn't even know how long. I realized on that suddenly eternal flight how much I had taken for granted: How close my mom was if I needed a hug and a word of encouragement. What a blessing living just two rooms over from my dad was. How much I loved spending time with my sisters every day, even with the annoying things they sometimes (okay, *always*) did. And how much I would miss all of those little things while I was away.

After crying for a solid dozen hours, I remembered something my dad had told me. He said, "Remember who you are. It's going to be great. You're going to have a wonderful experience." It was hard to believe that sitting there with my face wet and my nose running harder than I ever ran on the track, but remembering his voice lit a little candle in my heart. I could stop silently sobbing and only have a stray tear or two fall down my cheeks.

I wish I could say that the little fire grew and grew until by the end of the flight I was triumphant and excited about the year before me. But that wasn't the case. The confidence of my father gave me the quiet strength to face adversity rather than cower from it, but it didn't remove the adversity. I was still scared to death, and I still missed my parents.

So here's the thing. Everyone, no matter how old they are, is going to need a hug from their mom. That never changes. You always need your family. And your friends. And being so far away from them—maybe this goes without saying—it's not possible to go be with them. I couldn't go home for a long weekend, or for a holiday break, or anything. I didn't really know how hard it

EVERYONE,

no matter how old they are,
is going to need a HUG from their

MOM.

would be. Trust me, I knew it would be hard. You can't really prepare yourself for it until it happens. But you can choose, like I did, to not let it paralyze you.

When I finally arrived in Salt Lake, my track coach was there at the airport to pick me up. I was grateful he was there, until he opened his mouth and I could understand about 25 percent of what he said. All I remember from that night is sitting in the car, exhausted, eyes puffy, my head aching from crying, trying to keep my eyes open, and also trying desperately to understand what he was saying to me. My first thought was, *This is going to be rough.*

By the end of that forty-five-minute car ride, I was even more exhausted mentally, and I was so glad when he dropped me off at my host family's house. I lived with them for one week until I found housing. Their adorable, wonderful children helped me feel more settled into Provo in that first week than I thought was possible. Those kids made things so much better than I could have imagined, and I am so grateful that they fully accepted me, no questions asked. They played games with me, wanted me to sit next to them at dinner, and they were endlessly patient with my bumbling English. I am forever grateful to them. I was almost sad to move out into my dorm the next week, but I was glad to have a place of my own. That is, until I got there.

Chapter 5

BYU

I quickly learned that not everyone is as unconditionally accepting and understanding of language differences as an eight-year-old. As a result, I found myself in my dorm room a lot. It was really lonely for a while. I know some of you have been on missions, but this is a completely different experience.

Can you imagine living in a foreign country with very little prior education in the language for the foreseeable future? Not only that, but also being expected to study at a collegiate level in that language that you don't know? Make friends with people in that language that you don't know? Try and feed yourself in that language that you don't know? All with no family within a two-thousand-mile radius?

Let me tell you, it was so freaking hard.

I remember one day that was particularly hard. I had been in my room all day, and I was really frustrated with how difficult it was to learn English and communicate. I had just finished Skyping with my parents, and I was wiping away my tears, when right then I made the decision to be all in or all out. There was no in between. No one could make the decision for me, and since no one was reaching out to me, I had to be the one to reach out.

Easier said than done.

Learning English slowly but surely was one thing, but constantly trying to fit in with a new culture? That was a constant battle. I was constantly trying to be like everyone else, thinking that would make me more approachable or make people want to be my friend. I tried to talk like them, act like them, and dress like them (except I was *not* going to wear flip-flops). It was exhausting, to say the least. Track team made it better, because I had instant friends. And I was busy with it immediately.

I lived in Wyview, but I moved to a different apartment pretty quickly. I was still in Wyview, but in a different apartment with way better roommates. My first roommates and I just didn't click. We didn't get along at all, and we had really different views of the world. Their habits were so unlike mine. It was almost impossible to share a room with them. My mom kept the house clean, and they would leave the dishes in the sink undone and the living room all messy. My house was super social and always had things going on, and they just did things without me. We were different on every level.

My apartment was close enough to campus that I could walk until winter hit. That first week, I got lost more than I would care to admit, but I always got where I was going eventually. Who knew the campus was that big?! I didn't, and I had even visited! I swear they added stuff between the time I visited and when I finally got there to attend. School hadn't even started yet, thankfully, so I had time to get adjusted before I had to worry about being late to classes.

After I got the hang of getting to campus for the most part, my coach introduced me to a couple of upperclassmen who were on the track that day. They invited me to do a workout with them—no biggie, right? I had no idea what to expect, but I knew I couldn't say no. This was part of being all in. I decided to take every good opportunity that came my way, and getting invited to a preseason workout with seasoned athletes would be good, right? That's what I was hoping for anyway.

In reality, I was terrified. How would I measure up with them? Would I disappoint my coaches? The day of the workout, I got there way earlier than the rest of the team. My mouth was like a desert, not because of the Utah heat but because of the nerves.

While I was shaking off the jitters at the start line, I saw a girl across the track. She jogged up to me and introduced herself. Her name was Chelsea, and she

The sky is never falling . . .
things will work out;
they **ALWAYS** work out.
Stay focused,
accept everything as perfect
and keep moving forward
toward the direction of your goals.

—Mike Basevic

No Limits, Mastering the Mental Edge
(Smashwords Inc., 2013)

was a freshman too. She was also going to be on the track team. She offered to warm up with me that day and every day after that. She was yet another angel in human form, this time a girl from California far away from her family like me, sent to make me feel just a little less lonely and invisible. After that day, Chelsea and I became best friends. Over time, she became like another sister to me. We were attached at the hip, yin and yang. We did everything together, and she helped me so much. We studied together, and I wouldn't have gotten through it without her.

When I moved out of my first apartment in Wyview, my new roommates were much more welcoming and always invited me to church and social events. They always kept me in the loop and went out of their way to help me feel included. They would always help me with schoolwork, and if there were rules that I didn't understand, they would take the time to explain them to me. I guess I should explain that.

One day, I went to class in a tank top. I sat down and put my books on my desk and waited for class to start. Then I started to feel it. Eyes staring at the back of my head. My shoulders. My back. I thought, *Why is everyone staring at me?* One of my friends walked in, immediately came to sit by me, and told me, "Hey, Fatty, you need to put a cardigan over that." I had obviously signed the Honor Code, but I clearly didn't understand it. And it was that way with a few things. I was at track practice one day, and we were doing an ab workout that was just killing me. We finally finished, and I shouted a word to express my pain and discomfort. Everyone on the team burst out laughing! I had no idea what was happening. My friend Chelsea told me, "Fatty, that's a swear word!" I was so embarrassed and said, "I'm so sorry! I'm so sorry! It's not a swear word in Sweden!"

I was so lucky to have friends who could show me the ropes. Chelsea continued to be a godsend. She lived in the dorms *and* had a car, so she was basically the coolest. She would pick me up in her sweet ride, and we would hang out with her friends. I gained so many friends just because of her, because she saw me and reached out to me. I felt like I had friends or knew people from all over. I'm pretty social, like my dad, but I can be shy, so the leg up was awesome. I had some advantages at BYU; I was different. I stood out. I mean, black girl, from Sweden, named Fatty. Pretty unique, right? I used it to my advantage. Starting conversations can be hard in any language, let alone one you aren't comfortable in, so I tried to be as natural as possible. Here's how introductions normally went:

"Hi, my name is Fatty!"

"Hi—wait. What was your name again?"

"It's Fatty!"

"Yeah, that's what I thought you said, but I wanted to make sure! I didn't want to offend you or anything! So, is that short for anything or . . . ?"

Boom. Now you have a conversation.

I love introducing myself to new people because it's so hilarious. What is even better, though, is watching my friends introduce me to their friends.

"Hey! This is my friend, Fatty!"

"Uh . . . what?"

Cue mortified look. I live for those moments.

So English was easier socially than I was expecting. The language barrier was mostly in classes. That first semester, I sat in the front of every classroom with my big dictionary open next to my notebook on my desk and prayed every day that I would get something out of the lesson. It was a struggle to just comprehend the lecture. I know now that most students feel this way, but they weren't looking up every other word in the dictionary like I was. Some days I thought I knew exactly what I was being taught; other days I had no idea what was going on. It was incredibly frustrating because I knew I was smart in Swedish. Or French. Or Spanish. But English? Not so much.

If the classes had been taught in any of the languages I knew, I wouldn't be having so much trouble. I fantasized about the classes being taught in those languages and watching my classmates, who seemed to get everything so easily, struggle the way I was struggling. It was hard some days to remember that I really did know things—in every other language but English.

Another huge blessing was being an athlete—not just because of the needed mental break from classes, but a lot of athletes had classes together, so we could study and prepare together. My teammates helped me the most when I had to practice oral presentations. I *hated* presentations. I was never confident in speaking. I got away with not giving talks in sacrament meeting for five years, because I said, "I can't speak English." Which was . . . 25 percent true? Whatever, it doesn't matter. I don't have much of an accent normally, but when I get nervous, my accent comes out nice and thick, which was super embarrassing. And what was even worse about presentations was using PowerPoint. I *loathe* PowerPoint. I hated those little animations that everyone used on their slides almost as much as I hated standing there and talking.

Taking tests was even worse than classes and presentations because whatever language they were written in wasn't English. I was surprised to find that my classmates thought that too!

"What the heck? We didn't learn this in class!"

"He said that the test would be based on the textbook! This wasn't even in his lectures!"

"Oh, good! I'm so glad it wasn't just me!"

But God had my back. I was amazed at how all of my teachers were so willing to help me before and after class. I loved my teachers at BYU. Without them, I wouldn't have made it. Sometimes the professors let me take tests in their offices with the TAs so that they could explain questions if I didn't understand what they were asking, which was *so* helpful.

All in all, that first semester was a total blur. After every class, I was just exhausted. My brain was mush from trying to absorb so much information and translate it all. I was constantly trying to figure "What did we talk about?" "What was this assignment?" "When is it due again?" But for all that stress, I felt the Lord's hand every day. Sometimes I came out of my class or the testing center passing and sometimes I failed! But I have a degree, so don't judge me! You win some, you lose some.

I remember that first semester I registered for an accounting class. Don't ask me why—I have no idea! The second week of classes, right before you could drop, you get this huge packet full of problems. I had absolutely no idea what any of it said. I sat at that desk feeling that gross panicky feeling in my chest. There were so many words and numbers on it that my eyes were swimming. I came home and just sobbed. "How am I going to do this? There is no way!" I was a student athlete, so I had tutors, which was great. They honestly saved me on many occasions, but they could only help me so much.

I went to the teachers and told them, "I cannot do this. I'm good at math, but this is another language."

They helped me as best as they could, but I dropped the class. And not a moment too soon. It was an immediate relief, but I still felt like a failure. I called my dad, crying.

"Dad, I cannot do this! I have to come home!"

"It will be okay! You can do this. One day at a time. Just talk to your teachers."

That was part of my problem. I felt like such a jerk, saying, "Um, I don't really speak this language," because there were other international students and none of them were complaining. I didn't want to be the only one complaining. But I figured if I didn't say anything, the professor would never know. So I swallowed that embarrassment, and I went to them. I was amazed at how willing they were to help me, work with me, invite their TAs to help me. They went above and beyond to help me understand and feel comfortable with the material. My mom was right. If I did my part, God would do His.

I was improving, though, every day. I just couldn't see it. That improvement is so hard to see in the day to day, though. That's how it always is, in fitness, the gospel, school, whatever. You can't always see the small strides you are making each day, how you are getting better each time you try to do what the Lord wants you to do. And then suddenly you look back several years later, and you can say, "Wow. I have really come a long way," and not have felt the progress for a second. All it felt like was struggle. That's why it is important to cut

"**GROWTH** is painful.

Change is painful.

But nothing is as painful
as staying stuck
somewhere you don't belong."

—Mandy Hale, *You Are Enough*

yourself some slack but always push yourself to do more than you think you can.

So I kept going to class with that dictionary. And over the course of the semester, without even realizing it, I needed it less and less. And even if I didn't see my growth at the time, I knew without a doubt that God did, and He wouldn't leave me hanging. So I kept doing my part and trusting that He would do and was doing His. And wouldn't you know it, I had my highest GPA after my first year at BYU!

So even if your experience isn't exactly like mine, we're all going through something that we're not sure we'll make it through. And we wonder, *Does Heavenly Father really have my back?* Maybe we wonder that because we put ourselves in the situation that we're in. By our own actions, we are struggling. *Does God have my back even when I made the mess that I'm in?* Maybe it's because of something that happened to us or was done to us. Maybe it was something we wanted that now we're not so sure that we can handle. *Does God have my back even when I doubt a plan that He confirmed for me not long ago?*

The answer to all of these questions is a resounding YES!

He has your back always. You are His child.

There's a scripture that I love and the concept of it is, *Could a mother forget her nursing baby* (see Isaiah 49:15)? Absolutely not! It's unthinkable. Even more unthinkable is the idea that the Lord God could forget you, His spiritual son or daughter. How could we even think that the Savior could forget us? Wasn't He the one who said, "I have graven thee upon the palms of my hands" (Isaiah 49:16)? Yes! He is the same!

Our Heavenly Father and His Son will never give up on us, so don't you dare give up on yourself. You have a heavenly support system that will never, ever fail, and you have an earthly one too. Never forget them either.

My earthly support system was my family, but they were back in Sweden. So, I had to find a new one, because I was struggling hard at BYU. I think I've told you that enough times, right? I found a new family in my track teammates and coaches. I am forever grateful for that automatic sisterhood, and now I completely understand how people say that the friends you meet in college will be your friends for life, because that has absolutely been true for me! I spent countless hours with them. We ate, fought, made up, laughed, cried, sweat, bled, and sometimes did absolutely nothing together. We grew so close that I couldn't remember how I had ever lived my life without them in the first place. I had finally found my place. And I was the happiest that I had been since coming to America. We were in the middle of fall practice, and we worked hard and busted our butts on the track, and we played just as hard. We went to football and volleyball games almost every weekend, stayed up super late, and had so much fun just being together.

During this time, I realized that Americans just have a thing for celebrating stuff! They seriously celebrate anything and everything, stuff I had never heard of before. Best Friend Day, Talk Like a Pirate Day, Star Wars Day, Donut Day—I mean, the list goes on and on!

But my all-time favorite of all the ridiculous "holidays" in America is Chocolate Chip Cookie Day. I mean, how can you not love that day?! It's right up there with the bigger American holidays in my book. The silly ones were fantastic, because I could celebrate them just fine. It was the national holidays that were kinda rough for me sometimes.

The first one I dealt with was Thanksgiving, which was the first time in a while that I felt lonely again, because a lot of my friends went home to spend the holiday with their families. It was my first time feeling left out at BYU in the sense of "I don't get to go home to *my* family." And that was rough to deal with. I had been able to hold the homesickness at bay while my friends were around and we were busy having fun, but it all came crumbling down that week. I let that one negative thought affect me and make a huge downer of my whole week. Remember how my mom said, "One day I won't be there"? Well, this was it! She wasn't here, and there was no one to take me in. This was just the beginning, and I had a choice again to either hide and be sad or get out and go with the flow.

I think that a lot of times we decide the outcomes of different things or choices in our own minds in advance, which result in us feeling down. Like, "I'll never get invited to parties," or "I don't get asked out on dates, and I'll never get married"—stuff like that. Maybe we subconsciously do that to lower our expectations in case these scenarios *do* happen, because we're afraid of being let down, so we let ourselves down in advance before anyone else can do it to us.

But when we do that, many times we end up limiting what God *will* do, because we limit what we are *willing* to do.

I learned very quickly to step out of my comfort zone in order to thrive. I learned that while I may have felt like the only student on campus who had family far away—or even the only foreign person at BYU—that was never the case. There were many at BYU in the same situation as me. For all the other situations, there's at least one person out there dealing with something similar to you.

I was surprised to find that I had a lot of friends who couldn't go home for Thanksgiving for different reasons, and they were all as bummed as I was! I wasn't alone at all! If I had locked myself away in my own sadness, I would never have reached out and found people I knew who were feeling just as lonely and left out. But I did.

And you know what? We did our own thing for Thanksgiving, all of us loners together.

THINK ABOUT THIS:

**CLOSING THE DOOR
AND LOCKING YOURSELF IN**

WON'T CHANGE ANYTHING—

LITERALLY AND FIGURATIVELY.

—Richelle E. Goodrich, *Slaying Dragons* (Smashwords Inc., 2017)

That moment made me reflect on my childhood and my mom's constant invitations to others to come to our house. Strangers became family that way, and that was exactly what was happening to me.

Since then, I have lived in America for ten years, and this last year was my first time making Thanksgiving dinner on my own. Now, what does that mean? It means that for nine years I have spent the holiday at the homes of various friends—friends who became family to me. All because I refused to stay miserable in my room and reached out like my mom before me. I know it's asking a lot, believe me, but don't be afraid to be vulnerable! Don't be afraid to be you just the way you are!

Thanksgiving is really the calm before the storm, because right after the break are finals. That first year of college truly revealed all of my insecurities and also my strengths. I learned that I really am capable of anything. I just didn't necessarily feel that way during finals.

Once again, I prayed harder than I had ever prayed before. I was praying all the time—for anything and everything—but mostly to just understand the material I was studying. You know that feeling when you've stayed up late every night and studied so hard, and then you take your test and it feels like it's in a different language? Well, that was my reality every time!

But God is there, prayers are real, and He is listening. I somehow passed, and I breathed what felt like my first real sigh of relief in four months. I had done it!

All my friends were scheduling their finals so they could leave and go home to their families for Christmas. Unfortunately, I was left behind again since I wasn't able to go home that year. That was even harder to swallow for me than Thanksgiving had been. Christmas is my absolute favorite holiday, and we do it big in our family—so big that we celebrate it twice: once on Christmas Eve with our immediate family and then again on Christmas Day with anyone and everyone. We dress up, dance, laugh, eat so much food that we could die, and make some incredible memories. I was going to miss out on that for the first time in my life, and that really crushed me.

One day I was in the locker room studying when my friend Chelsea came up to me.

"So, Fatty, what are your plans for Christmas?"

"Oh, nothing really. Just hanging around here. I can't go home for Christmas this year so—"

"Come spend it with me and my family. We would love to have you."

She didn't even hesitate. I cried tears of joy, right there in the locker room. I spent my favorite holiday not with my family, but with my best friend's family, who became like a second family to me after that trip.

I called my parents right after I finished hugging Chelsea. I was still sobbing when they finally picked up.

"Fatima, are you crying? What's wrong? What happened?"

"Nothing bad! Chelsea's family is letting me come to their house for Christmas! She just offered to let me stay, out of the blue, when I said I couldn't come home. I won't be spending it alone!"

My sweet mother then said, "I knew you would be taken care of. God never leaves His children hanging."

For He hath said,

I will *never leave thee,*

nor *forsake thee.*

Hebrews 13:5

Chapter 6

Ready, Set, . . . GO!

Running track at BYU was amazing. Our coaches were great at team building. We were a team before everything. A lot was expected of us because we represented our team and we represented BYU. I fell in love with track again while at BYU, but I still dreaded fall every year.

Track was a whole different ball game (see what I did there?) in America. And college track was super rough. My coach always said I was lazy because I would do the bare minimum. I hated long distance *and* I was a lazy sprinter, so that wasn't helping.

But then I got married, and I changed my mind-set. I thought that if I wanted to improve my times, I needed to work harder. Run longer. I needed to be a leader too, to the younger kids. My mind-set changed from *What can I do just to get by?* to *This is what I have to do to get what I want.*

Senior year, I became a team captain, so I was even more of an example. Not only was I called upon to be a leader for the team, but I was to be a help for the coach too. The team captain not only leads the team on the track and carries out the coaches' directions, but they are also the eyes and ears of the coach. They report back with what's going on with the team, who's fighting with whom, and all of the news that keeps a team running smoothly, on and off the track.

I did a whole lot more than I thought I could running at BYU. My coach in Sweden wanted me to run 200s and 300s, but I didn't want to. I hated those races. But when I changed my mind-set, I started running them in my junior year, and I shaved so much off of my times. It was incredible how much I was improving by listening to my coaches! They'll roll their eyes when they read this, I'm sure. But they know. Coaches know what they're doing and what they want you to become. And they know what you have to do to get there, no matter how crazy it might look to you!

I did a lot of different exercises. Everything was different. I had to change it all up. I had a good base to work from, but looking back at pictures, I say, "Wow, I wasn't as lean back then!" There's a huge difference in my junior year—I got really lean. I never had the Cannon Center plan, so I cooked for myself and wasn't tempted by the fatty, unhealthy food they had there. As a result, I stayed pretty lean. When I had been at BYU for a few weeks, my mom said, "I hope you were paying attention to all of the cooking I've been doing!" I thank my lucky stars that I was!

Chapter 7

The Storm

After my freshman year, I got to go home for the summer! I hadn't seen my family in almost a year, and I couldn't wait to hug them and be around them. I had so many stories to share, so many experiences from school, track, church, and just life in general. On my way back to Sweden, as I sat on the plane reflecting on my first year of college, I couldn't help but feel immense gratitude. As I looked back on the year, I recognized my growth. How far I had come and how proud I was of myself for getting where I was, spiritually and mentally.

I was so excited to see my parents and younger siblings at the airport. Those hugs were worth the wait! I couldn't wait to get home and make dinner with my mom and sleep in my own bed! But my excitement was short lived. Once we got home, my parents informed me that they had left The Church of Jesus Christ of Latter-day Saints.

This was a decision they had made, and they expected all of their children to follow suit. My happiness and excitement at being home withered inside me at those words. I was in shock, honestly. That was just not on my radar at all. But I collected myself, and the words that came out of my mouth were, "Okay. I respect your decision, but I will stay."

The three months being with my family that I was looking forward to so much turned into something way harder for me. Well, it was difficult for all of us. It was the first time I was going in a different direction from my parents, and I never imagined that it would be about the Church. My parents were nice about it, but we didn't always agree on everything. My dad and I had a little bit of a harder time navigating these changes. I love my dad, and we are a lot alike, so you can maybe imagine how hard it was to not be on the same page as him.

All of a sudden, I was getting ready to go to church by myself. Instead of taking up a big pew, I was all alone. That year at BYU had tested me in ways I couldn't have imagined, but those months at home were a completely different kind of hard. They were some of the hardest I faced. Not only was it hard because I had to go to church alone, but it was also hard because of the questions coming from other members. It was hard because of the judgments. It was hard because I literally had no answer, and I had a hard time figuring out the why.

My own testimony had grown so much over the year that we were apart. I witnessed miracle after miracle happen in my life. I watched how bishops took care of ward members and how miracles came from fasting as a ward. I saw how praying and serving others not only blesses them but us as well. There was no denying it for me then, and I just could not fathom how I could have gone so far down the gospel path in one year while my parents traveled equally far off the path in the same amount of time. I still don't know all of the reasons, but I know that family is forever, no matter which way on the path they are headed.

I am sure that you know someone who has left the Church. Religion is always a topic that is hard to talk about because everyone has different opinions. It can be easy to get offended or hurt by others' opinions and views. I had conflicting emotions and confusion about how to act. I didn't want to be the cause of problems or contention, but that seemed to be where I always ended up. I had a lot of questions. How can I find the balance with my dad? How can I be okay with their decision and keep my standards as well? It was hard to explain a sensitive subject. When I would go to church alone, people would ask, "Where's your family?" I felt like I was fifteen again, full of questions with no way to answer any of them.

"I sustain myself
with the love of family."

—Maya Angelou

"Charity is the pure love of Christ" (Moroni 7:47).

I love this quote, and I had to read it often, because it was the answer to my questions. The application was sometimes the part I got stuck on.

I mentioned that my dad and I are very much alike—which can be good but means he's sometimes hard to get along with. My whole life my dad and I had always gotten along really well until this happened. I knew how hard it was for me to be leaving him behind, in a sense. I am sure it was equally hard for him to watch his daughter do her own thing. Even though I knew it was the right thing to do, I always felt bad. It seemed like religion would always come up, and each time my stubborn self would leave feeling angry. I was angry because I felt like I wasn't being understood. I was angry to even be in this situation. I felt like I was the reason for contention in the family. Why was I feeling this way when I knew I did the right thing? Where do I go from here?

Things got harder when I went back to Utah. That father-and-daughter closeness that we once had was slowly fading away. The daily calls that we once had became not as often. Something needed to change, and it needed to change fast. I didn't want to be causing problems just because we had different gospel-related views, and I was frustrated! During one of many conversations that I had with my former bishop about my frustrations, he told me something that I needed to hear and remember: "He's still your dad, Fatty."

"Yeah, but he doesn't understand."

"Yeah. But he's still your dad."

What struck me about this bishop was his incredible capacity to love. He loves his wife more than anything. He loves his children more than anything. He and his wife, Pam, have raised five amazing children, and I like to say I am their adopted daughter. (I mean, if I get to come to family dinner on Sundays, I am pretty much family!) And he is the example of the pure, Christlike love that I wanted to follow. So I tried. I'm still trying. I don't always succeed, but when I could be angry, I try to show love instead.

There is no such thing as too much love, and I was sometimes too stubborn to see that. To anyone who has family members who have chosen a different path, remember to love them no matter what. But not with just any kind of love. Love them with the pure love of Christ. While it might be easier to be angry and retaliate, love trumps all, and you will never regret showing love rather than anger. It was hard for me to do things and progress because it took me so long to accept the circumstances. When I accepted that things were the way they were and that my parents were the way they were, I was able to choose to not let the circumstances get in the way of my love for them, and everything changed. With any relationship, if we want it, we have to take care of it. We have to work for it, cultivate it, and handle it with love.

Now, family to me is more than just the people you share DNA with. Family is also the people who are constantly around you, those you love and freely serve. You may not talk to these people every day, but when you do talk, it's like nothing has changed. They uplift, encourage, and inspire you to be better each day. And I found those people by swallowing my fear and insecurity and getting out of my comfort zone. I made each interaction about making someone else feel something rather than thinking about myself. I tried to be like my mom, or like my friends Chelsea and Rakeb and notice when someone needs something.

Not too long ago, I messaged a girl that I didn't really know. I felt prompted to message her that Heavenly Father knew her and what she was going through. I was prompted to tell her to not give up. But I pushed it away. I literally said aloud to myself, "I don't know her! I can't just say that!"

But it kept coming, and I finally did it. I was so surprised when she messaged me back and said, "You have no idea what that means to me. It was exactly what I needed." I was glad that I didn't keep ignoring that prompting and that I pushed past my initial discomfort and reached out.

I saw her sister a few days later at the grocery store, and she immediately started crying. That made me a little nervous at first. But then she came up to me and said, "She is going through some serious personal struggles, and she is just trying to get back on her feet. She really needed to hear what you said." I had no idea! But I was so glad to have listened to the Holy Ghost.

I learned to be grateful for a lot of things in my time at BYU. I learned to accept my differences, use them as strengths, and never apologize for them. I didn't go there to fit in any more than I went there to wear flip-flops. (Seriously, you couldn't pay me enough.) I am a black girl from Sweden, a track athlete and fitness buff, and my nickname is Fatty.

I am the girl who called insects "animals."

I am the girl who will mispronounce things all the time because English is hard!

And I decided in my freshman year to be all in.

To be me and own it.

And I've never looked back.

You are not here to be like anyone else. You were sent here to this earth to be *you*! Don't change yourself hoping to get the approval of others. Don't act differently because you want to be like the "cool kids." You won't really get their approval anyway. You won't be happy, and you'll just be exhausted because you'll constantly be trying to measure up to someone else.

God made you to be you! And He is a perfect God. He gave you your strengths because you are able to help others in a way that only you can. He gave you weaknesses so that others could strengthen you and you could learn from them.

You are NOT here to be
like anyone else.

So whatever it is that is going on in your life right at this moment, embrace it. If someone in your life has decided to go a different path, embrace them. Love them. Love them hard, because life is too short. Stay true to what you believe in and be all in. Be you! Just as you are. I promise you that you will be happier and that people will love you just for being yourself.

Trust me on that one. Because if I hadn't been comfortable being myself, I never would have met Ben.

Chapter 8

Night and Day

"You're going to go to Utah, meet a boy, and get married!" Every one of my friends said this before I left Sweden to come to BYU. As for me, I hadn't even considered that as a possibility.

Being a student athlete leaves very little time for dating. I did a lot more "hanging out" than dating, to be honest. And that was completely fine with me. I was busy and had an awesome group of friends, and we all had so much fun together. There was no pressure. It was nice.

But Utah has a way of pressuring you.

I wrote myself a letter when I was thirteen about the kind of man I wanted to marry, where I wanted to be in life, and what kind of mother I wanted to be. I forgot about that letter when I left for BYU because I had hidden it away somewhere. But the contents were always in the back of my mind. I dated before I went to BYU, and some during my time there as well, but it wasn't a serious commitment like my thirteen-year-old self thought it would be at that time in my life. Isn't it funny how we have a plan for ourselves but Heavenly Father has something completely different planned out?

It was in my sophomore year, right after I had moved to a new apartment right by campus and had new roommates. I was in an awesome ward and had just gotten my first calling (FHE mom, if you must know)! Having a calling in college was one of my favorite things. It helped strengthen my testimony, and I got a little glimpse of the behind the scenes of church. It also strengthened my testimony that we are all called for a reason and that the most important calling in the Church is the one you have right now. You are needed there right now. I was needed as FHE mom, and I loved it.

Like mother, like daughter, my apartment was the hangout spot. My roommates and I always had things going on at our place. Whether it was a movie night, game night, or some other party or event, we always had friends over. As I watched my friends and roommates meet boys and go on dates while I sat at home, I literally thought, *Well, I'll never get married, and I have to be okay with that.* I thought I would never find my person who would take me to the temple.

That may seem like an extreme reaction, but let me break it down for you. As silly as it may sound, I didn't look like the typical Utah girl. I didn't dress, talk, or act like most of the girls who were getting asked out. And on top of it all, I didn't want to think about marriage at all because I was nowhere near ready.

Remember what I said before about deciding your own outcome in advance to avoid being let down? Yeah, example number one: Fatty's dating life.

After a while of being stuck in that rut, I had to face facts. How can I ever be ready for marriage if I'm not constantly working toward it? So I dated. I dated someone I thought was a great person. I thought he had the same goals as I did, but as time went by, I saw a lot of differences in our goals. I kept hoping for changes and that by being a good example I would see those changes. Instead I was dragged down. I was invested in a relationship where it was hard for me to grow as a person, and all of a sudden I realized that I had lost my usual happy self. I wasn't so happy anymore. I watched myself struggle doing simple tasks. I got really good at faking it, but I was never able to make it.

There were definite red flags. The paragraph above is practically red flag city. But I was in denial. Heavenly Father gives us red flags and signs, but it is up to us to acknowledge them. If you were to ask me today, I could list the signs that I chose to ignore because I thought I was doing the right thing. I thought that things would

Heavenly Father gives us
RED FLAGS AND SIGNS,
but it is up to **US** to
acknowledge them.

get better, that they would change. But I had to come to terms with the fact that I cannot change someone without them being willing to change. I cannot control anyone's actions. The only thing I can control is myself.

That realization didn't come overnight. I struggled for months to come to grips with the reality that I needed to let go. The struggle was taking its toll physically, emotionally, and spiritually in every way imaginable. I wasn't doing the things I knew I needed to be doing. It's amazing how far off track we can get when we stop doing the small and simple things. I spent so many nights on my knees praying for strength and clarity. The answer was right in front of me, but for some reason, I had a really hard time accepting that Heavenly Father was right. After that, I had an even harder time finding myself again. Slowly but surely, I stumbled my way back. And not a moment too soon!

During one of our customary Sunday game nights, a new guy came to play. His name was Ben Dedrickson. I noticed him, but I was dating someone at the time, and I found out later so was he (though he likes to say that he wasn't). My first impression of him was how hilarious he was! He made us all laugh so much, and we loved the spirit that he brought to our apartment. My second impression was that he was *tall.* He had just gotten back from serving a two-year mission in Detroit, Michigan, and he had the best stories from it. He came into not only my life but also my roommates' lives at the perfect time. He and I became instant friends, and we talked about anything and everything.

It didn't take long before I felt comfortable enough with Ben to share some of the things I was struggling with. I was so glad I did, because he listened to me and gave me the advice I needed from an eternal perspective. That added perspective was all I needed to realize what I needed to change. I cannot describe the weight that was taken off my shoulders as I decided to rise again.

Sometimes Satan tries to convince us that what we are doing is fine when we know that it isn't. He tries to convince us that what we are doing is okay or that peoples' behaviors are okay when in reality they aren't. Do not settle for fine or okay, and do not live your life trying to convince yourself that you are happy when you aren't. Focus on your relationship with God, because He's the only way to real happiness. That's how I found mine, and I can tell you that if you try and do the small and simple things, blessings will unravel in your life like nothing else. Just wait and see!

I went home to Sweden again that summer, and it was a lot better than the year before. I loved the time at home, but I would be lying if I said I didn't miss Ben. So when I got back to Utah, Ben and I were inseparable. I remember thinking *Holy cow, whoever marries him will be one lucky girl*. Around the same time, I made a deal with Heavenly Father. I pretty much told Him

If you try and do the
small and *simple* things,
BLESSINGS will unravel
in your life like nothing else.

Just wait and see!

that whoever I dated next I would marry, because I was tired of dating!

You can see where this is going, right?

Ben and I hung out every day, so it only made sense for us to date, right? The only problem was . . . me. He was my best friend and I didn't want to ruin our friendship. It meant so much to me, you know? I know—I'm rolling my eyes too. Bless his heart, he didn't give up on me and my stubbornness. One day he said, "What better way than to date your best friend?" For some reason, that was it! It was like night and day from the last relationship I had been in.

I was so happy to finally be in the kind of relationship that made me happy. He encouraged me to be my best. It was all of those good things. Even better, I had made that deal with Heavenly Father, and I knew I was going to be the lucky girl who got to marry him. Score!

We dated for a year and a half, which is an eternity in Utah time, I know. I knew I wanted to marry him, but it was really important to me for Ben to come to Sweden, meet my family, and see where I grew up. It was a sacrifice, but he agreed to travel to Sweden (total sarcasm, by the way). That trip is still one of my favorite memories from college. We even had the chance to visit my sister's family in London on the way! My family absolutely loved him (how could you not?), and there was no question that he was meant to be part of the family. I chalked that up as a success.

As soon as we got back from Europe I was ready for him to propose! Just like that. Ben had plans of his own though. Let's just say that one month of waiting felt like three years. I'm not a patient person, and when I want something, I want it right away. So for a whole month I was suspicious of everything. That boy couldn't even tie his shoes without me thinking, *This is the moment!*

Needless to say, I was ready for that knee to drop. We *finally* went ring shopping and everything was looking up, and then . . . I had to get my wisdom teeth taken out.

There are three things that I hate more than anything: the dentist, rats, and the experience of finding something hard when chewing something soft. Now, I know it sounds weird, but listen. Bread is supposed to be soft, right? Whole-grain bread with all those little grains on the top? I'm gagging just thinking about it.

Okay, now that that's out in the open, we can move on.

It was a Friday, and I was feeling pretty good despite the fact that I had just gotten my wisdom teeth taken out a few days before. Ben had taken such great care of me all day, from getting me food to simply keeping me company. All our friends were going to a party next door, so I told him we should too because I was feeling fine, but he had different plans. He was very persistent about me getting in my comfy clothes and resting. I, on the other hand, felt fine and didn't need to rest! I can be pretty persistent too.

He suggested we go to the temple and walk around. That was our thing. We'd drive to the Provo temple, sit in his truck, and talk for hours. I wasn't even slightly suspicious, so up we went at 11:00 p.m. As we got there, the workers told us we had a little time before they had to close the gates. We walked, talked, and laughed, and then he got real serious.

"What would you do if you looked up right now and there was a helicopter with the words 'Will you marry me?'"

I laughed. "Yeah, right. As if that would happen!"

We turned around a corner and sat down on a bench. He then started saying all these sweet and romantic things like:

"I love you so much, and I cannot imagine my life without you."

"You are the best thing that has happened to me, and I can't wait to be with you forever."

He got up, grabbed my hand, and said, "Well, we better go, because I'm pretty sure we have been here longer than we were supposed to be."

Um, what! Can you even believe this guy? Here I was 99 percent sure he was about to get down on one knee, and suddenly we needed to go. I was a little bit disappointed, but I held onto his hand and kept walking. Until suddenly, he stopped, turned around, got down on one knee (FINALLY) and said, "Fatima"—he only uses my full name when he's serious—"I love you with all my heart and . . ."

The rest is blurry, because all I remember were tears of joy and me answering "YES." We kissed (by that, I mean made out), and then got locked in the temple grounds. We laughed some more, jumped the gates, and called our families to tell them the news.

We planned for a three-month engagement so we could be married before track season started. That is not a lot of time to plan everything, and I was feeling the stress! Leading up to our wedding, things started to get hard. Isn't that how it always happens? You know what they say, when you're about to do something right, Satan will do everything in his power to break you and stop you.

When I was young, I promised myself that I would have a temple marriage. But not all of my family could enter the temple. And they were halfway around the world. Planning a wedding with half the wedding party on another continent was no easy task. Doubt and fear crept into our minds about the big decision we were making. There was so much going on, we were disagreeing on a lot of things, and it was just *hard*!

In the African culture, there are a lot of traditions revolving around marriage and even some before you get married. Obviously, all countries have different traditions, but in Congo and in my family we have some traditions that we have followed for as long as I can remember. The bride's family gives the future husband a list of things he needs to get for his in-laws. The gifts are like a token to show your love and respect as you take the daughter from her father.

I know it sounds different, and because Ben wasn't raised that way, he had a hard time understanding it. Quite frankly, I had a hard time with it too, because we weren't raised exactly that way, and I didn't really agree with it all. But it's a tradition! Are you still with me? We had a lot of arguments about it as I tried to explain this tradition to Ben. It was a lot for him to process.

One tradition we didn't know about that was to take place after the wedding was that we would be given an envelope with an amount of money in it for us to start off as a married couple. Because we didn't know about it, we disagreed a lot about finances and money. In the middle of it all, Ben's mom came over one day. She asked us, "What is the most important thing for you both? Do you love each other? If the answer is yes, then everything else will fall into place. The little details of flowers and colors and caterers don't matter. What matters are the covenants you will make inside the temple."

That made me feel better, because I was really struggling with the fact that my family wouldn't be able to be present in the temple for our sealing. The fact that my family couldn't be in the temple actually made the decision we were making clearer and even more important.

"May we ever choose the

harder right

instead of the

easier wrong."

—*Thomas S. Monson*

"Choices," *Ensign*, May 2016

I was making the choice to be sealed to Ben for eternity. I was doing that for us and for our future children, so that they would have the blessings of our covenants too. I knew it was right, and when I knew that, the way forward was clear. In life, not everyone is going to like your decisions. But what really matters is doing what is right and what makes you happy. "May we always choose the harder right rather than the easier wrong."

As our wedding day got closer and closer, my family and best friend flew in from Sweden to help us prepare. They stayed with some of our friends, who selflessly opened their homes to these people they had never met. My parents asked what they could do to help and were surprised that we had a lot of things taken care of already. They were in awe at how many people were already helping us. I caught my mom tearing up as we were working that day, because she couldn't believe the love everyone was showing to our family.

Even so, there was still a lot of prep to do, and I needed my mom to do it. If you know anything about African weddings, you know that there is a lot of dancing and a ton of food. My parents stayed up almost all night cooking and preparing the food. I also had not tried on my wedding dress (ever!) because I wanted to wait and do it with all of my sisters there. So, naturally I waited until the day before the wedding to have that moment, and I will say that it was worth the wait and the risk.

The day of the wedding came, and Ben and I headed to the Salt Lake Temple to be sealed for time and all eternity. Even though my family couldn't come inside, the feeling and the Spirit on the temple grounds was undeniable. The moment Ben and I stepped out for the first time as husband and wife and saw our waiting families—I have never felt happier than I did in that moment. I saw my mom, tears in her eyes, arms outstretched, waiting for us to embrace her. It was one of the best hugs I have ever had in my life. I then cried as I hugged each of my sisters and my best friends. My dad was being a typical dad and recording the whole thing with his camera, but what he said to me when he finally embraced me will stay forever in my heart.

"My little girl, I am so proud of you."

Easily one of the best days of my life. A day when all of my families—blood, chosen, and newly acquired—came together to celebrate the formation of my new eternal family with Ben. I was over the moon all day.

We left the temple to have a ring ceremony, officiated by Bishop Welch. It was small and intimate, with our closest family and friends, and it was everything I could've asked for. It was so special for me, and I knew it meant the world to my family. My bishop was so thoughtful. His remarks were short and sweet, and he made the ceremony very sacred and special to us.

We had a reception afterward, and that was the big, blowout party! Food, dancing, and speeches—all that good stuff! By the end of it all, Ben and I were exhausted. All we wanted to do was go home and sleep. And that's what we did. Day 1 of eternity—check.

Just a note, because I get asked all the time. Has being in an interracial marriage caused us any problems? We are incredibly lucky that the answer is no, at least not directly. We have always felt the support of both of our families since the beginning of our relationship. Unfortunately, we do live in a world where racism is still a problem no matter where you live. My biggest fear is not for myself. It is watching my children have to deal with racism. The thought of them being exposed to that makes me want to cry. I know I cannot protect them at all times, but I know someone who can. So one thing that I will always teach my children is that we are all children of God, no matter where we come from or what we look like. We are all unique in our own ways and perfect just the way we are. It all starts in the home, teaching kids what is right and teaching them to love one another like Jesus loves.

HATE cannot drive out **HATE**.

Only *love* can do that.

—*Martin Luther King Jr.*

"Where Do We Go from Here?" as published in *Where Do We Go from Here: Chaos or Community?* (1967), 62.

Chapter 9

READY, SET, STOP!

Not long after our wedding, I was sitting on a plane flying back to Utah after my last track meet as a BYU track athlete. My emotions were all over the place, and a million thoughts were running through my head. As I chatted with my coach, he asked a simple yet fateful question: "If you could choose one thing you would want to be in life, what would it be?" Without hesitation, I answered, "A mother."

But it wasn't always that way. Ever since I was a little kid, I dreamed about running in the Olympics. That's every athlete's dream, isn't it? I dreamed of representing Sweden and going pro. But as time went by, I grew older, and it became clearer and clearer that Heavenly Father had a different plan for me.

Despite my easy answer to my coach, the adjustment to actually being pregnant was a process. Now, I will say up front that I'm one of those weirdos who loves being pregnant, but with my first, I had no idea what to expect. And that was hard for me, especially as a collegiate athlete, in the best shape of my life, with a very regimented workout schedule, being told that I would have to stop. That is something I have never done: stop. I am always going, so that was a tough one to process for me mentally.

I was track. That was me. It was a huge part of who I was, and I had to figure out who I was now that I couldn't participate in track for the time being. That means growth, and growth is good! But it's also scary to let go of everything you thought you knew about yourself and essentially start over.

I had to ask myself some hard questions, such as "Who am I if I can't run? If I can't compete? What if this derails my running career? Can I be okay with that? Even if I can't compete, exercise is still my passion. What does that passion look like now that so much has changed?" It was a huge adjustment in so many more ways than I expected. And going from looking a certain way all my life to seeing all of the different changes was hard at first. I had no idea how my body would react at the different stages, and that uncertainty was no fun.

But once I learned the flow of it, I learned to love being pregnant because of the miracle I was creating. I loved the way my husband looked at me as I was growing our child. I loved feeling the first kicks, watching my belly do weird things as the baby was moving. I didn't love having to wake up and pee all the time though—ha!

We put a lot of pressure on ourselves as women to maintain our bodies and fitness while pregnant so that we can still look hot in our heels for as long as possible. But that's not the best focus to have, at least not for me. Your focus should be on your health and the health of the baby, and if that means sweats and a topknot most days while you're surviving real life, that's what it looks like. That's what it looked like for a lot of my pregnancy anyway, and I loved it! When I could finally look past the added pounds and the fact that none of my clothes fit anymore, I came to the realization that my body was doing what it was meant to do to bring my children safely into our family. That changed my whole perspective from gaining weight to growing a baby.

One year into our marriage, we brought Noah into the world. By all accounts it was the wrong time. Ben was taking his hardest classes in his program, and he was insanely busy trying to graduate on time. In fact, the day after Noah was born, Ben had an organic chemistry test! How's that for stress? We often talk about that time in our life together and wonder how we did it. And the conclusion we always come to is that we couldn't have done any of it without Heavenly Father's help. He brought people into our lives to help us when we needed them. He blessed us with strength to keep going even when we were totally exhausted!

And for me personally, He helped me to be still. And then, when it was time, He helped me get back up and run again. That was always my plan, by the way.

After I had Noah, while I was still in the hospital if you can believe it, I told Ben, "I still want to run track. I'm not ready to hang my laces up or put my shoes on the shelf. Running is a part of me that I don't want to give up yet."

His answer was simple and sweet: "If that is what you want, then I support you 100 percent."

And that was that. I made the goal to run in the Swedish championships, which would be held a year from the day Noah was born. So my reality was not being still for long before I was back up and running, slower than my usual pace, but still out there running and trying to get back into track shape. I found myself running metaphorical hurdles rather than running normally, because motherhood was just not what I expected it to be. I didn't really fully appreciate the gap that would exist between my dream and being a mom and how that would change what my normal routine and prep would look like.

It was a constant war of priorities.

Noah and Ben were, of course, my biggest priority, but getting back in shape to meet my goal was a high priority too. And that goal was so much harder to achieve than I had envisioned it.

See, in my head, I would just train the way I always had, and pretty soon, say a month or so, I would look the way I did before I had Noah and be back up to speed.

That is so not what happened.

I remember running around the track one day, super frustrated that I was still getting winded. I was also sweating sooner than I expected, and I said aloud to myself, "This is *way* harder than labor was!"

There were so many days that I came home with my legs feeling like cement and jelly at the same time and I fell on the floor because I couldn't make it to the couch. I mumbled into the carpet, "I can't do this anymore." I wanted immediate results, and when they didn't come immediately (because that's literally impossible), I thought I was failing. I questioned if it was meant to be and wondered if it was time for me to quit.

How often does this happen in our lives? We set goals like running a marathon, losing weight, or starting a business, and we expect immediate results, just like I did. Because of this, we don't honor the small steps of progress we are making along the way.

The breakthrough for me was how I talked to myself. You don't talk to anyone more than you talk to yourself. You're in your own head all day, telling yourself things, psyching up to do things, and psyching up not to do things. You're always communicating, whether you realize it or not. I realized that I was almost always negative when I talked to myself.

For example, after a hard workout that used to be easy, I would think to myself, *I just can't do it anymore because I'm a mom. My body is different, and it will never be like it was before.*

When opportunities to do things would come my way, I would immediately brush them off. *I can't. I'm a mom. Noah's nap time is right smack-dab in the middle of that play/movie/activity, so I can't go.*

Or, *I can't go out and make new friends. I'm a mom. I don't have time for that. I barely even have time to shower.*

And the crazy part is that I listened to that voice. It was me after all, and I was only saying what I was already thinking, if that makes sense. So my self-talk was defining me. If I said I couldn't do something, you can bet that I didn't do it because I already knew I was going to fail.

It was a long time before I realized, *Wait! I don't know that! I don't know that I'm going to fail. And I can do things even if I had a baby. I just have to work my butt off until I get where I want to go.*

That type of thinking seriously changed everything. You'd be amazed at the power of positivity and a can-do attitude. Rather than resign myself to future failure, I empowered myself for future success. That was the option I chose, so I worked until I achieved it. It wasn't easy, but that's not what I asked for or agreed to. I agreed

Rather than resign myself
to future failure,

I EMPOWERED MYSELF
for future success.

to do whatever it took to get what I wanted, and if that meant working twice as hard to get it, that's what I did.

We still lived close to campus, and I was still training with the BYU team. Our friends who lived nearby did so much to help us while Ben was busy with school and I was training. They stepped up when we needed them, and I will be forever grateful for that. I looked around and saw how much work everyone was putting into helping me achieve my goals. I saw Ben getting up early to take care of Noah while I went for a morning run, even though he had stayed up late the night before doing homework. I saw my sweet in-laws coming to the rescue anytime we needed their help. I saw friends of ours who had their own busy lives and goals of their own stop and look after Noah for an hour or two so that Ben and I could have some much-needed time to ourselves to recharge. I saw members of our ward bring meals for us when Noah first came home. And equally meaningful, we got phone calls from family and friends from all over the globe to encourage us, love us, and offer their support. That meant just as much to us.

My first real taste of return on all that investment was my first track meet postpartum. I ran so well that it was one of my best openers to date. But I wanted to keep going and keep getting better. I set smaller goals that would help me make those improvements. The next thing I knew, I was in the best shape of my life, something I had never thought possible again. It all started with mental and spiritual strength—the strength to believe that I could do it. And after that, it was (metaphorical) cake. (Except not really, because it was still incredibly hard, but let me be dramatic for a second, okay?)

After going to that meet and focusing on those small goals, I was on a solid path to the Swedish championships. What had seemed like a long, hard slog was a very real and present possibility.

Noah's first plane ride was a doozy of a fourteen-hour flight to Stockholm for the championships. He took it like a champ and only cried most of the time. When we landed it was so surreal. There I was, back home, but a completely different person. When I went back with Ben, that was different. Then, I felt a little older and wiser but still myself, more or less. But this time I was coming back with Ben and the child we had made together. We were both so fundamentally changed by that and the year we had together that I felt like an older, much cooler Fatty that day. It's weird to think that a place can have seen so much of your life. It sees you grow up, leave, and then come back more and more sporadically. Each time you come back, you are older, more experienced, and more mature. It's crazy. But I was there to run a race, which reminded me that underneath it all, I was still the same Fatty I've always been, only with a few more experiences under her running shorts' waistband.

When I stood on the start line at the Swedish championships, I was filled with pride that was like a balloon in my chest. It swelled and filled me up until I was almost bouncing down the track. It was not just because I had made it and done what I set out to do, but also because I looked up and from that start line could see my husband and child cheering for me. The moment I saw them in the stands, I knew that no matter the results, I had made it. I had achieved my goal. I had succeeded.

I ran that race with everything I had. And I made third place. When I stood on that podium watching my nation's flag wave and I got to hold my son as the crowd was cheering us on, that was one of the most powerful moments of my life. I'd wanted to give up many times. But I did it, and it was worth all of the pain, frustration, worry, stress, sleeplessness, and cramps. I. Did. It.

Whatever your journey is, focus on it. Focus on your own progress, not on the lane and the person running next to you. If someone is going faster, that doesn't matter. You are only in control of your own journey, so you might as well focus on you. If you're a mom, it doesn't matter how old your kid is. You don't have to use the mom card as a "get out of jail free" card forever. Use it as the fuel you need to motivate yourself to do what you have always wanted to do and to prove who you are. The steps you take now are the steps that will eventually lead you over the finish line.

You can have more. You can keep your identity and gain a new identity as "mom." There will be things you have to give up in order to have more, but don't be afraid of that. You have to be willing to put in the time and effort and use the right tools to accomplish your dream. In the process, you are teaching your kids that their identity matters, their goals matter, and the only thing keeping them from success is themselves. There is nothing wrong with acknowledging your gifts and saying that you are good at something. God gave us talents to cultivate on this earth. In fact, I think He specifically said not to bury them. So dig up those talents. Brush the dirt off them and take them to the next level.

When we have kids, we tend to push away our dreams and forget about our gifts. The problem with that is that kids move out (fingers crossed), and the further your talents and gifts slip away, the harder they are to find. There is absolutely nothing wrong with putting 100 percent into your kids. That's beautiful, and maybe that's your gift, but for me, I need to do the things that make me the best mom. One of those things is running, and for a time it was competing. Now? It's investing in other moms, making them feel loved, appreciated, and *seen*. I want to share this lesson in self-love that I've learned in my own life, because I've lived without it, and it's a dark and lonely place to be in, especially with little lives relying on you.

I started by reclaiming the things that used to make me feel less. When I was younger, I absolutely hated my arms. I mentioned way back at the beginning that kids made fun of me because I looked manly. Well, my arms were the manliest part of me. I was more muscular than the rest of the girls in my class, and that made me really self-conscious. I wore shirts with long sleeves to hide them whenever I could. Then, when I went to college, my arms served me well. Those arms that I had been ashamed of all my life? They helped me hold myself up in the set position at the starting line. Those arms helped me carry all of my grocery bags into my apartment *in one trip*! I was a strong, independent woman, and I didn't need any man to carry groceries! Those arms helped me hold others tight when they needed a hug. And those same arms helped me hold all of my babies when they were born. I could go on and on, because my arms have done a whole lot of things, and I should be (and am!) proud of them, not ashamed.

Self-love isn't selfish. When we hear self-love, we think manicures, pedicures, and #treatyoself. But at its core, it is more than that. It's about working on loving the person we see in the mirror and extending them the same love, patience, and understanding that we are so willing to offer the other people in our lives. Even if we look in the mirror and don't feel it right away, we can know exactly what we need to do to get there. And

SELF-LOVE

is not

SELFISH

for me, that means way more than just focusing on the physical things.

After the Swedish championships, we went back to the States, and I started training for outdoor season. Ben finished up his last semester and got his undergraduate degree in exercise science. As he was finishing up, he had also applied to the physician assistant program to a couple of different schools. As we were waiting for any potential interviews, Ben got a job as a cardiac rehab therapist at Utah Valley Hospital. This was a huge blessing for us because that income helped us throughout that year. As we were waiting for that, I was still training and getting ready to travel with BYU. I would usually leave on Thursdays and come back on Sundays. This was definitely the hardest part of me competing again, leaving my family behind every weekend. Almost every weekend I was lucky enough to travel with BYU and compete for my Swedish club. After two months of competing, I flew to Sweden by myself to compete, and I was gone for three weeks. This was the hardest and longest three weeks of my life. I knew Ben's support was necessary, or I wouldn't have left. Although Ben fully supported me, being gone from him and Noah absolutely killed me. We FaceTimed every day. Thank heavens for technology, and I am so grateful for my in-laws, who helped watch Noah when Ben was working.

It was extremely fun to compete and be back with my family and track family in Sweden. I had multiple track meets and got to travel to some of my favorite places in Sweden. It felt like I was sixteen again, traveling with my track club and competing. While I had a blast, my heart was still in Utah with my family. As I prepared to head back, I remember being on the plane gathering my thoughts. I felt, for the first time, completely satisfied. My goal was to compete again after having Noah, which I did. I accomplished way more than I ever thought was possible. I had filled that cup all the way to the brim, and I felt ready to hang up my shoes. I needed that trip to realize where I was needed even more, which was at home with my family. It was time to close that chapter of my life and support my husband in his new career. My child needed his mom, and my husband needed his wife, and I needed them to feel complete.

It was a strange yet satisfying feeling, because not once have I looked back on that day and regretted my decision. I left on a high. I did the impossible, and I did it as a mother. Don't ever let the mom card bring you down. You can do whatever you put your mind to as long as you are willing to work hard.

Closing one door opened up many others. I got pregnant with Olivia, started doing photography, and was introduced to the influencer world. I started blogging about fitness while pregnant and sharing the different workouts I was doing. I was lucky to be introduced to some local bloggers and became good friends with them. I loved sharing the different exercises I did on a daily basis and slowly but surely started growing my social media. After Olivia was born, I was fortunate to have done a couple of photo shoots with Freshlypicked, happybaby, and a famous photographer in Utah. They truly helped get my name out there. Without really knowing it, things just kind of grew from there.

Life got busy in a different way, and it was exciting. Ben was put on a waiting list that first year and reapplied the next. He was interviewed by all the schools he applied for. We did a lot of road trips together and made many, many memories. I wanted to go to each place, because after all, I would be home with the kids and I wanted to make sure it would be somewhere family friendly. When we came to Arizona, we both knew as soon as we got there that this was a place we wanted to move to. Ben just had to nail that interview. This was actually his second one, because he was put on their waiting list the year prior. We knew that they usually call pretty quickly after to inform you if you got accepted or not. So you can imagine our drive back to Utah. We were constantly staring at Ben's phone.

As soon as we were out of service, we were those people holding it up just to have one bar appear. I have always had the mentality of "If this is where Heavenly Father wants us to be, then we will be." It wasn't long until Ben did get the phone call, and we were told that he had been accepted to the physician assistant program. Our prayers had been answered, and we were thrilled.

"I hope you realize that EVERY DAY is a fresh start for you. That every sunrise is a new chapter in your life waiting to be written."

—Juansen Dizon, *Confessions of a Wallflower*

With the help of Ben's parents and brother, we packed up all our belongings and were about to start a new chapter in Arizona. Olivia was only a month old, and I was truly excited for a change of scene for our family. I was excited for a new area, a new ward, new friends, and for Ben to start his program. Like anything new, moving was obviously hard on us. Saying goodbye to my in-laws was a lot harder than I thought. I have truly been blessed with amazing in-laws. We couldn't have moved without them. I cried way more than I thought I would. I mean, at this point, you probably know that I cry a lot—ha!

Starting a new chapter is always hard, no matter what point you're at in your life. It is different for everyone, but at the end of the day, it is still hard. When we got to Arizona, our dear friends from college had moved there, and they came to help us out. It was good to see familiar faces and to know at least a couple of people. Nevertheless, we still had to start fresh and new. This was the first time other than his mission that Ben was away from his family, so it was a lot harder on him than it was on me, because I had already done it.

This is where we learned to rely on each other. This is where we were forced to grow as a couple and as parents. The years of him being in school were some of the hardest ones for us. Anyone who has a spouse in school while being a stay-at-home mom knows the struggle. Not only was it hard to send Ben to school every day, but since we moved at the worst time possible, it was also extremely hot. Going to the park like we usually would do in Utah in the summer turned into going to the pool or staying inside. This was a huge adjustment for me. I am not a typical indoor person, so being cooped up inside almost every day with a three-year-old and a newborn was a challenge.

One of the greatest blessings of being part of The Church of Jesus Christ of Latter-day Saints is Relief Society. It is meeting at church every Sunday and deciding that you will meet someone new. While it might be hard to be the new person, it can also be a great blessing. You are forced to step out of your comfort zone, introduce yourself, and put yourself out there. Don't take that opportunity for granted. Dare to sit next to someone new, and dare to introduce yourself to other people. If you want to have a friend, you first have to be a friend, right? This was never easy for me, but I knew I had to do it if I didn't want to be lonely. Whenever things got hard and I found myself feeling sad or down, that usually meant I hadn't gone out or done something for myself. So I made a promise to myself to do something every day with the kids, whether that meant to go get the mail together, let Noah run around, go to the pool, go to the indoor play house at the mall, set up a play date, or go to a friend's house.

Speaking of friends, can we talk about them for a minute?

Why is it so hard to make friends? Especially as an adult? I swear it is way harder now than it was when we were younger. I know I'm not alone in this. I want you to know that you are not alone in it either. You are not the only one feeling like it is hard to find your people. You are not alone in wanting a couple of great friends in your life. We all yearn for solid friendships—friendships that you see other people around you involved in, or on social media. Do not let social media fool you. Not everything on there is real.

Get out of your comfort zone and reach out to people. I know, I know—easier said than done. But I sincerely know this to be true.

Chapter 10

Be Still

It was the beginning of a sort of chaotic time in the Dedrickson house! Ben had three weeks off from school before he started his second year of the physician assistant program. We originally were just going to take it easy and have some fun as a family, but then we decided last minute to go visit our family in Utah. When I say last minute, I really mean that.

The day before we were due to leave was the most chaos I had experienced in a while. Packing for kids is a nightmare. When you're single, you know how you pack tons of clothes for a really short trip or vacation, convinced that you'll need all of them, and then you wear the same pants and maybe three shirts the whole time? Yeah, that's the opposite of how you pack for kids. Kids are messy little gremlins that seem to consider it their mission to soil every bit of clothing that you put on their tiny little bodies. You have to pack for a month, no matter where you go or for how long, because they will inevitably find the nearest body of water and fall in or splash in every muddy puddle in the state you're visiting. And let's not forget the bodily functions. Poop, pee, snot—you name it, they wear it! To say I was frazzled would be an understatement.

The day of our departure, we left after Ben got home from school at around 1:00 p.m. We were eager to just get to my in-laws' house, so we strategized on how to make the least amount of stops possible . . . while driving with a newborn. Newborns mean many, many feedings and diaper changes. Basically, we made quick stops to get rid of the stinky evidence of our road trip ingenuity, like using the middle console as a changing table. Noah was three, and he's always been a champ in the car. We were hoping that he would be an example to his sister, but she was not a fan of her car seat. She cried most of the way from Arizona to Utah. I don't know about you, but a crying baby in the car gives me horrible anxiety. It just stresses me out and makes me feel powerless. But you roll with the punches and do what you have to do. We wanted to get there quick, so we drove through the night. And by that, I mean Ben drove most of the way (thanks, babe!) while I tried to keep the kids happy.

At around 1:00 a.m., Ben's eyes were getting droopy, so I said, "We're so close. Why don't you let me drive?"

"Are you sure? I think I can make it as long as you talk to me and keep me awake."

"I'm sure. I slept for a while, so I'm good. You sleep."

We pulled over to the side of the road and switched drivers. We were just about the only car on the road, so it wasn't too hard to get back on the highway. It was just so late. We were already in Utah. We just needed to go a little farther and we were there! At around 3:00 a.m. was when all chaos started coming through the seams.

We were all so tired—tired as in sleepy and also just tired of being in the car. The kids started waking up and getting really fussy. Olivia in particular. At one point, she just started screaming at the top of her lungs and wouldn't stop.

"Ben, just take her out of her car seat and hold her. We're only twenty minutes away."

Not even five minutes after I said that, a huge semi-truck entered the highway and merged into our lane. I couldn't swerve to get away because we were flanked on the left side by another semi-truck.

We were sandwiched between two enormous hunks of metal going seventy miles per hour!

I tried to speed up and swerve past the car in front of us, but I bounced off one of the semis, over corrected, and we spun out.

That was one of the only times in my life that I felt like time slowed to a standstill. I couldn't comprehend what was happening since it all happened so fast. I looked back at Ben. He was screaming my name. I looked at Ben and my babies and thought, *We are dead.* I was sure this was it, and we weren't going to walk away—until we hit the median, and we hit it hard. Everything crashed and crunched until we finally jerked to a stop. There was a long pause. Then I heard my sweet Noah's voice, "Mom? Are you okay?"

I lost it. Through hysterical sobs, I turned around in my seat and pulled Noah into my arms and squeezed him as tight as I could. I looked into the backseat more closely, and the only side of the car that was damaged was the side opposite of Ben and Olivia. We were all alive! We were not only alive but also uninjured!

I cannot even begin to tell you how lucky and blessed we felt that day. Our guardian angels were definitely there to protect us. We walked away from that wreck with mild whiplash.

I'd like to say that I never took anything for granted ever again, that the new perspective I gained was with me all the time, and that I never again lost my patience with my kids. But that's not true. I did get better. I learned to more fully and truly cherish our time together as a family because I saw how fleeting it is. I made a goal to be more intentional with the people I love the most. To pick up my kids more often than I pick up my phone.

"Your phone won't feel bad if you don't pay attention to it.
It won't care if you haven't played with it in a while.
It won't mind if you don't hold it.

YOUR CELL PHONE will be small forever;

your children will not."

"Your Cell Phone Won't Feel Bad," Kim Uliana,
https://kimuliana.com/2018/09/23/your-cell-phone-wont-feel-bad-by-kim-uliana.

Something less awesome changed in me since the accident too. I was scared a lot more. I was scared to drive. Every time I got in the car, my heart would beat a little faster. Over time, I got over that, but I still get anxious every time I see a semi, and I make sure to keep my distance. I'm not sure if I'll ever really get over it, but with each day and each positive experience I get more and more confident. What I'm saying here is that bad and good exist in the same experience.

I came away from that experience with incredible insights and also some incredible anxiety and fear. It is possible to experience something and say, "Wow, I learned something really valuable that I'm glad to know, but I never want to go through that again." And that's a totally valid feeling! Change and growth are not always pleasant to experience, even if the lessons are invaluable.

I personally like to look at change as an opportunity for growth. Sure, that growth may not be the most comfortable, and it may be downright painful, but I would prefer that over staying stuck somewhere I don't belong. Putting what I preach into practice isn't always the most graceful, but I do my best.

We moved to Arizona from Utah for Ben's physician assistant program, and that was a hard adjustment for me. But I grew and did my best with it. It was hard and painful at times, but I did my best to bloom where I was planted. I think I did a pretty good job, if I do say so myself! And when it came time for Ben to graduate, we knew we were moving back to Utah. A month before graduation we were looking at houses. We found one that was like a dream come true. It had everything we wanted in a house *and* it was in the area we wanted to live in. Score! We would be super close to family and friends. We were thrilled and couldn't be more excited to get out there and start our new chapter.

But just to be sure, we said a lot of prayers to confirm our decision and to ask for comfort about our plan. One night, Ben was working a night shift and I had just put the kids down for the night. I closed their bedroom door and stood in the hallway reading over the housing contract. And there it was. Like a burr in a sock, picking at me. Something about the contract didn't sit right with me. I tried to push it away. "It's just jitters, Fatty. You're just nervous about making such a big step, that's all." No matter how I tried to convince myself, I knew that wasn't the truth. And after a couple of days and staying in contact with the owners, Ben and I both had that feeling. You know, that feeling where your mind is telling you, "Yeah! Go for it! It's perfect and it's your dream!" and your heart is saying, "No. God has a different plan for you"?

I'm not going to say that I hate that feeling, but those moments take a lot of faith and courage to move on. I knew we were doing the right thing in not buying the house, but I was sad because we were right back to square one. I felt like just building a house there, on square one, since we seemed to be there so much. Now we weren't even sure that Utah was the right choice. But then, not even a week after we turned down the house, Ben got two different job offers in Arizona. Coincidence? I think not! We didn't want to put all of our eggs in one basket, so we stuck with our original plan, hoping that something would open up in Utah too.

Two days after Ben graduated, we loaded all of our things into storage and drove back to Utah with my in-laws. Again, my in-laws are saints and have helped us move twice now! Ben still hadn't committed to any of the offers he got in Arizona, and still nothing in Utah, but we went anyway and had an amazing time. We stayed with Ben's parents while we planned our next move, and it was so good to watch my kids strengthen their relationships with their grandparents and their cousins. That was so important for us. We talk about that time often, how we were able to slow down, be still, make memories, and have quality time as a family.

But our paradise couldn't last forever, as much as we wanted it to. The clock was ticking, and we (really just Ben) needed to make a decision. We didn't like it, and we avoided it for a while, but deep down we knew that we needed to go back to Arizona. This change was probably the hardest for me, maybe because mentally I was so ready to move back and be by our family again, especially after experiencing how wonderful it was those few weeks. Or maybe it was because I was so sick of the heat and excited to experience actual seasons again! Honestly, we were all sick of the heat. I was sick of it the most. Maybe it was because our kids were getting older, and we wanted them to grow up with their cousins and friends. At the end of the day, and after all the maybes in the world, we knew Arizona was where we needed to be.

Chapter 11

Fear Not, I Am with Thee

As much as we wanted things to happen our way, we knew there was a much better way, and, ultimately, that was the way we needed to go. We had a plan! A plan we really wanted to work out. Was it a good plan full of good things? Yes! But there was a better plan under our feet the whole time. We were just ignoring it while we were partying in Utah. Lucky for us, we are in great (and very patient) hands: God's hands. It can't get better than that!

We moved to a completely different area in Arizona, which meant new neighbors, new parks, new people, and a new ward. It was hard for me again because there I was, back at square one. We lived fifteen minutes from our old house, which may not seem like much, but it's long enough for a toddler (or a sleep-deprived mom) to fall asleep in the car. All of a sudden, places that had been really close and convenient, like Target, were really far away. I had a really hard time with the adjustment. Not just because of Target (though, let's be real, that's a serious problem), but because I was the new kid again. And it's way harder to be the new mom on the block than the new kid in school. But I had made the decision in freshman year, so I just had to reaffirm: was I all in or all out? Someone is always going to be the new person, so why not me? And change means growth. So I was all in.

This new area was what you could call "established." The people living there had lived there for years. I assumed most of these moms had their own "village" and weren't interested in welcoming newcomers. Some did, but a majority did not.

Here's the thing, we often assume that we know what other people have or need. We psych ourselves out before we even know their situation, and when we do that, we miss out on major opportunities.

Momming is hard. Whether you're a new mom or have five kids, it is still hard. Let's be real. It's always hard. Do not be afraid to reach out and step out of your comfort zone. Do not assume you know other people's stories. Finding a mom village does not have to be difficult. We are the ones who make it hard.

It was in the middle of July. We got a knock on our door, and our sweet neighbor who was pregnant at the time had locked herself out of their home. Her family was out on a walk around the neighborhood, and she needed to come inside while her husband figured out how to get in. We had only seen each other a couple of times, so this was our first time actually talking. I forced myself to ask questions, to be all in again. You see, I am convinced that because of that day and how I made an effort to get to know her in that small amount of time, we just clicked. Today her family are some of our closest friends that we love dearly. Some of you might think, "Well, that was easy or lucky," or "I am awkward, and it is hard to make conversation." A lot of people think I am outgoing because of my Instagram. It really has been a struggle, but it has taken a lot of learning and practice to go out of my way and be more social.

Having an Instagram where I am able to share my voice, story, and day-to-day life with my followers made it a little easier for me to connect with people in Arizona. Since I started blogging in Utah, most of my connections were there, but the beauty of being an influencer is being able to connect with people all over the world. I never in a million years thought this was going to be a source of income for us. In fact, I was just happy receiving cool products that I loved, especially baby items, because those are expensive. We were poor students, so that was a blessing in disguise.

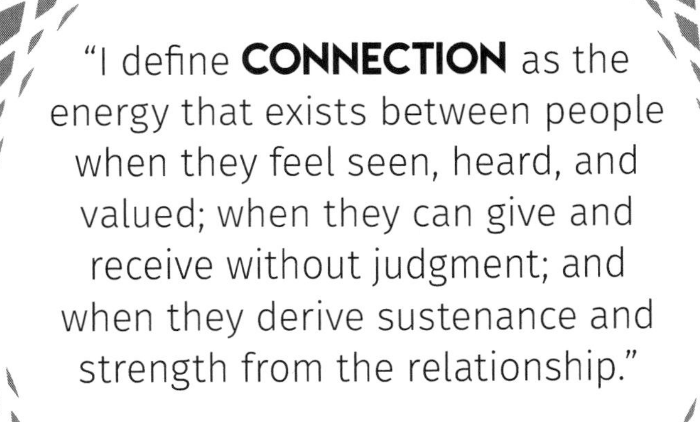

"I define **CONNECTION** as the energy that exists between people when they feel seen, heard, and valued; when they can give and receive without judgment; and when they derive sustenance and strength from the relationship."

—Brené Brown,
The Gifts of Imperfection

I was invited to an event, and I was thrilled, but then I got so nervous because I knew nobody! The thought was terrifying to me, and going to an event filled with other influencers and other business owners scared me. What do I do with my hands? Should I bring my baby as my safety blanket? Who will be there? Nobody knows me, so maybe I should just stay at home?

So many questions were going through my head, but I decided to put my big-girl pants on, and off I went. I met so many people. Literally every single person was new to me. The best thing about this event was that I learned to network and form relationships with people I probably never would have otherwise. A simple hi can go a long way, and it did for me. A simple invite to an event can open up so many other doors, and that is exactly what happened to me. My Instagram grew to be something more than just sharing fitness. It became a place for me to share my motherhood journey. It was a space to share spiritual experiences, my love for clothes, and uplifting thoughts.

Social media has given me a lot of positives.

I have made some of my really good friends through social media, because we could relate to each other and decided to meet up. The rest is history. I mean it sounds a little crazy as I am typing it, that I was willing to meet up with a complete stranger only because I trusted them through our conversations via Instagram. It *is* a little crazy, but it happened multiple times. Usually by meeting one person, I was automatically introduced to more people.

I have been able to build a community of moms, and I truly feel a connection with a lot of you! How amazing is it that although we might all be in different states, we have this app that helps us connect with each other? I learned that when I share my beliefs and real-life struggles, I connect more and more with other women. Who knew being vulnerable on the internet would help other people? This is where I want to address F R I E N D S.

For a long time, I thought to myself, *How am I going to form the kind of friendships I had in Utah? How am I going to get solid and real friends again, the kind of friends that know you're hungry without you even saying anything?* Does it happen over a day? Nope! Does it take time? Absolutely! Is it a one-way street? Heck no! We have to make the effort and continue to do so even when we get shot down. I think that is the hardest part, being shut down, because we build walls and think, "What is the point?" Does that sound familiar to you?

Every time I got attached to someone here, they moved! I am not joking. Three girls that I became super close to ended up moving away. Gosh darn it! Why does this always happen to me? Maybe I am not meant to have close friends—haha! Okay, that is a little dramatic! But I hope you see my point! I know a lot of people, yet I feel lonely. Every single one of us needs at least one friend. At least one person that you feel connected to. I heard somewhere on a podcast that we all need a friend that covers these three areas:

1. **Consistency—**We need to cultivate friendships and consistently see each other, which totally makes sense. The more you see your friend, the more you want to be around them and the closer you will get.
2. **Vulnerability—**We need to be able to show our weaknesses and be open with someone without thinking we will be judged or attacked.
3. **Positivity—**I don't know about you, but we all need positive vibes in our lives. The world is already so negative, and nobody wants to be around negative people or someone who brings you down.

Can you think of someone on social media that covers these three areas? I can think of so many people! What about the consistency? With Instagram, we feel so connected to people that we don't even know because of the things being shared. When we are consistently scrolling and involved, it almost fills a void in our real lives. Can you now see why we feel lonely because these three areas are covered on social media but not in real life? So as a result, we feel lonely, even though we might know a lot of people. We spend too much time focusing on those friendships, because—let's be honest—it is so much easier to be behind the phone and type, which is why there's a huge problem right now with us being on our phones too much.

I was asked not long ago how I balance being a mother and having a business on social media. I thought I knew

"*Frientimacy*

is any relationship where two people

feel really **seen** in a way that feels

SATISFYING and **SAFE**

for both of them."

–Shasta Nelson

Frientimacy: How to Deepen Friendships for Lifelong Health and Happiness (Berkeley, CA: Seal Press, 2016), 32.

the answer. I thought it was pretty clear to me and that I was good at balancing motherhood and social media. Boy, was I wrong. Unfortunately, this is something that I have learned the hard way. It started with my husband pointing out that I was constantly on my phone, which created some unnecessary contention in our home. I fought it for so long and defended my phone and the time spent on it every time. This is where my pride took over. Instead of trying to understand him and where he was coming from, I was too busy arguing and trying to prove him wrong. A lot of it was because I was embarrassed or didn't want to face the fact that I was on my phone too much. I didn't want to give up something that I had worked so hard building.

The funny thing is, Ben never asked me to stop doing what I was doing. In fact, he has appreciated every sweat and tear that I have poured into building my community and my side business. He has always been a great encouragement. He even likes to call himself my manager. I was worrying about pleasing my audience rather than worrying about real-life things.

But this was my business, right? I had to be on my phone. Sure, but this business doesn't come first. I am a little embarrassed admitting this, but I truly didn't realize how much I was on my phone until my sweet daughter yelled, "Mom, put down your phone and play with me!" Gosh, was I addicted to my phone? Did I become addicted to Instagram and addicted to the likes and the comments? This is something I talk a lot about not getting sucked into. Did I just get sucked into it myself?

I am not going to lie: validation feels good. It feels good to hear that you have been missed or to have someone ask you how your day was. It feels good to be able to connect with strangers because you shared an experience you had. It feels good, but only for a little while. It is only temporal.

For me, I am still trying to figure out how to find a good balance. The first step was realizing that I truly was spending way too much time on my phone, which was causing me to miss out on the important things happening all around me. Have you ever found yourself getting frustrated with your kids because you just want to finish reading someone's caption? Or you need to post something, and you have a toddler pulling on you, screaming your name? Or you couldn't wait for Dad to come home so you could catch a break, but what you end up doing is getting on your phone to catch up with strangers?

I am guilty of doing all of the above. I am sure I can relate to some of you on this. Whether you have a business on social media or not, we go there to get something from it. Whatever it may be—because I am sure it is different for everyone—how easy it is to get caught up in the social media world and become addicted to or get too attached to our phones.

Chapter 12

Love Is Not Spelled C-O-M-P-A-R-E

I thought college was hectic. No, I really thought I was busy then. I laugh at that now, as a mother of three young kids. My schedule is hectic. It can be easy to say that I don't have time to go to this activity or serve at this event because that's right in the middle of Kingston's nap time, or, wow, that's really late in the day and the kids will be crazy. I have realized that everyone's schedule is a bit difficult, just in different ways, and I can't really use my kids as an excuse to not be social. I have social and emotional needs too! And constantly telling my kids not to hit each other in the face with their toys just wasn't filling that need for me. But I found a way to lessen that void with social media.

Social media has a lot of great benefits to stay in contact with family and friends. It's a great way for moms especially to feel like we're being kept up to date in others' lives. We live in a digital world where we can connect with other moms through Facebook groups, Instagram, and also neighborhood groups. These places help us connect with people we probably never would've met. I am a living example of that, like I have mentioned previously.

It can also help teach our kids to be friendly, to learn to play with new kids, and to be brave. If mom can be brave and make a new friend, so can they. Actually, my kids teach me way more about bravery than I teach them. These are skills that I know will be beneficial for them as they grow up.

There is a major downside to social media that we have to acknowledge, and that is comparison. When we compare ourselves to others, that is when we lose confidence in ourselves.

The comparison game on social media is so toxic, and it has been something that I am continually working on getting out of my life. But it's so sneaky that even when I think I'm good and feeling pretty good about everything, I catch myself doing it!

Not long ago, I remember sitting on the couch, scrolling through my Instagram feed (wasting time), and I automatically started wishing I had "this and that." This body. That house. That testimony. This confidence.

Insecurities are developed because we compare our **"BEHIND-THE-SCENES"** with everyone else's **"HIGHLIGHT REEL."**

Before I even knew it, I was going down that spiral of being ungrateful for what I had in my life. Comparison truly is the thief of joy. Insecurities are developed because we compare our "behind-the-scenes" with everyone else's "highlight reel."

A lot of the time when we start comparing ourselves with someone else, we don't realize how hard that person worked and struggled behind the scenes to get where they are now. We also most likely do not know that person personally, which is even worse. It is so easy to look at people's highlights and think that their lives are perfect. Their kids are perfect, they are traveling the world, and they have the perfect home, so they must be perfect. I promise you this: everybody has trials, big or small.

If we don't feel grateful with what we already have, what makes us think we will be happy with more? More doesn't mean better or happier. In fact, for me less means less stress and more room for joy. It means more room to breathe and enjoy those around me.

Here's the thing: there's always going to be someone who is prettier, better at cooking, better at crafts, better at singing, better at dancing . . . the list goes on and on. Just because someone is better than you at something doesn't mean that you aren't good enough. And it sure as heck doesn't mean that you can't do that thing! Mariah Carey is way better than me at singing, but my kids love when I sing them to sleep. Gordon Ramsay is far and away a better cook, but pigs will fly before my kids eat caviar. Actually, same here! You have talents and abilities to bless your life and your family. Just because they aren't the same or at the same level as some influencer online doesn't mean they aren't exactly what they are supposed to be. Nor does it mean that you can't yet improve and grow.

Your worth is not measured by likes, comments, notes, or followers but in your ability to love, support, encourage, teach, take note, and lead.

What should you do when social media gets under your skin?

Delete, delete, and delete!

Seriously, it's that simple. There's no need to follow someone who makes you feel bad about yourself. Nobody wants to be friends with someone who doesn't bring positive thoughts to the plate. Remove all that negativity from your feeds and fill it with accounts that are inspirational, fun, motivating, and whatever it is that you love. Then fill your own feed with that.

We were given a challenge from our prophet President Russell M. Nelson to do a social media fast for ten days. Actually, he had advised the youth to participate in a week-long fast a couple of months prior to this, and I never did it, so this time when he asked us women to do it, I knew I had a desire to do it. I knew I had some sponsored content that needed to be posted, so I told myself I was going to wait until they were taken care of and then start my fast. After two days of not doing the fast and talking to my friends who were on it, I was inspired to start mine. This was my busiest time as far as social media work, and I knew that if I didn't start now, something else would come up and I'd postpone it. So I deleted all my social media for ten days! When I tell you that this has been the best decision I have made in a long time, I am not overreacting.

From doing the fast, I have realized just how important our work is as parents, and more specifically, as mothers and nurturers in the home. This is the time my kids need me the most. They will not be this little forever. It is amazing how not being on social media has completely changed the mood in our home. I had more time cleaning, cooking, reading scriptures, playing with the kids, and so on. I encourage everyone to take social media breaks and literally remove the app for a period of time. Watch what happens to you and to the people around you.

Being all in is really the only way to go! Online and offline. Don't wait around for someone else to do it—you do it first. Be the first person to say hi to a stranger. Look at your surroundings. If you are at the park, chances are there's a mom just as lonely and lost as you are there with her kid. Go up to her! Ask her how old her kid is, where she's from, and what *she* likes to do. (I know it's not watching *Caillou*!)

If you want to see something beautiful, inspiring, or uplifting on your timeline, create it! Don't wait for someone else to do it. You can do it yourself! Compliment someone! Both in person and in the comments section. Compliments are nice wherever they come from. We should give them sincerely more often. If you are at church, dare to sit next to a new person. Don't let anyone sit by themselves. Dare to start conversations. Be involved in the community, callings, and events around you. Sometimes I think we put ourselves in these lonely situations because we are scared of rejection, but kindness never goes out of style. And in the stretching to make connections, even if you fail, you're growing and becoming more like the person you were meant to be. So stretch! Grow! Strive! Be brave. Go beyond what you thought you could do, because you'll never change your situation by doing the same things you've always done.

And don't forget to make time to just be still.

You go through big chunks of time
where you're thinking,

**"THIS IS IMPOSSIBLE.
OH, THIS IS IMPOSSIBLE."**

And then you just keep

— *going and going,* —

and you sort of

DO THE IMPOSSIBLE.

–Tina Fey

About the Author

Fatima is a mom of three and a lifestyle and fitness blogger. She was born in Sweden to parents from the Congo and grew up in a family of eight children.

Fatima came to the United States on a prompting that she really wanted to ignore. But she packed, moved to Utah, learned English (in that order!), went to BYU, ran track, met her husband, got married, and now has three beautiful kids. Currently, she lives in Arizona with her little family and organizes events to help women—especially moms—love, support, and celebrate themselves.

Scan to visit

stylefitfatty.blogspot.com